A Casual Traveler

"If you're looking for a great vacation, go to an all-inclusive resort.
If you're looking for a great travel adventure, go anywhere else!"

A Casual Traveler

"If you're looking for a great vacation, go to an all-inclusive resort.
If you're looking for a great travel adventure, go anywhere else!"

Edmond Gagnon

Acknowledgements

Thanks to all those people who have encouraged me to pursue this endeavor.

- -to those of you who have travelled with me and waited for me while I stayed behind to capture that "perfect picture"
- -to the people and fellow travelers I've met who have become my friends, subjects of my musings, or acted as an inspiration to me
- -to "my readers" for all the positive feedback on my travel tales
- -to Cathryn, who helped with the tedious editing process and has learned to "Give me my space" when I need to be creative and capture in words, our travel experiences.
- -to all my family and friends.....this book is for You!

Dedication

This book is dedicated to my mother, "Joan Marie Cecile," who passed before her time.

You taught me patience and perseverance, humility and humbleness,
integrity and ingenuity. You passed on your caring and creativity.
You told me I could be a leader, instead of a follower; that I could be good at anything, if I put my mind to it.
You are my inspiration.

I miss you mom!

Contents

Introduction 1

Missing in America 3

Coco 8

The Fugitive 11

The Walkabout 13

A Sensual Awakening 17

Bullets, Bugs, and Birds 19

The Hog and the Cow 25

Bus # 94 30

A Royal Tour 36

Mad Max and the Mud Road 42

Universal Language 47

Circus City 49

Eddie Murphy and the Golden Girls 55

King Cobra 61

Floating Junk 67

Lands of Lam 72

Fresh Beer 79

The Beach and the Sunset Bar 85

My Gym 92

Rocky Mountain High 99

On-line Dating 106

Goose Bumps.. 114

Contrasts 118

Doors... 124

Mendoza by a Landslide!.. 126

Tale of the Dragon 130

Freebird.. 137

North and South.. 140

The Train & the Tower 149

Breeze in Belize 159

Consider the Conch... 169

Princess of Belize... 171

Caye Caulker Critters.. 176

Pops' Island.. 181

In The Jungle.. 189

Southern Comfort.. 200

"To travel is to live"
– Hans Christian Andersen

Introduction

This book is my collection of short stories, and a few poems that describe and represent the last three years of travelling in country, and abroad. Some of my life's ambitions have been to meet new people, to try different foods, and to discover new places. Travelling has allowed me to do all these things. My adventures and misadventures have humbled me; I will not live long enough to even scratch the surface of the many places in the world I want to see, and visit.

My stories spent their infancy in the form of email that I sent to family and friends as I traveled. I've been lucky enough to see and do things that many others simply can't for different reasons. My intention in relating my musings is to put people in my place, so that they might share in my experiences. I received positive feedback from my readers saying that I had accomplished this goal, and they encouraged me to carry on. Some of my readers said I should consider writing a book, or publishing some of my stories. As any author knows, writing and publishing a book is no simple task; I do love a challenge though and I took on the project. With the exception of a brief history on the birth of my Wanderlust, these stories are about my travels after my retirement in January, 2009. My first two month journey to Southeast Asia was an eye opener and an inspiration for me to pass on my experience to others. I firmly believe that "Everyone has a story". I have come to understand that there can be a potential story in the every day events in our lives. For me, travelling opens my eyes and awakens my senses; I am more creative while on the road, and this trait has allowed me to share my passion with you.

Missing in America

Back Roads, U.S.A.

"I took the road less travelled, and that has made all the difference"
— *Robert Frost*

Maiden Voyage

One of the ways I satisfy my sense of adventure is by travelling the back roads of Canada and the United States. Like Clint Eastwood in "The Bridges of Madison County," I have searched for things and places lost in time, history, or just to "progress" and urban sprawl. The mode of travel I enjoy the most while wandering and exploring roads and places mostly forgotten, is my motorcycle. Although I have had some memorable car trips in the past, I find my motorcycle offers me more of a sense of freedom, with the added challenge of negotiating the winding and hilly roads that stitch together the colorful towns and cities that are strewn across our vast land.

My first solo motorcycle adventure was when I was 19 years old and I had two weeks of summer vacation to burn up. I was riding a 750cc Honda at the time and decided to head south to see how far I could get. I told my mom I'd call when I got "somewhere." I had a U.S. road map and some cash. This was well before mobile phones or GPS. I had applied for my first credit card, but had not received it in the mail before my departure. You could fill up your gas tank for a few bucks back then, and stay in a road side motel for under $20 a night. I brought a pup tent and sleeping bag so I could take advantage of even cheaper camping rates.

Without really understanding the difference between Interstate, U.S, rural roads, or highways at the time, I just crossed the border

3

from Windsor, Ontario into Detroit, Michigan through the tunnel and jumped on Interstate 75 heading south. Just crossing the border through the tunnel on my bike is noteworthy since they stopped allowing motorcycles through it many years ago. It was kind of cool listening to your exhaust pipes rumbling and echoing off the tunnel walls.

I quickly learned the pitfalls of riding on the big and busy highway when I was rear-ended in a construction zone in Kentucky. I managed to keep upright while being pushed down into the grass median. My bike received some minor damage that I was lucky enough to have temporarily fixed by a friendly gas station attendant. As if that wasn't enough to get my heart rate up; I was riding through Atlanta beside a tractor-trailer when it blew a tire. I thought someone had put a shot gun up to my ear and I was sprayed with pieces of flying tire debris. Fun times on I 75.

I made it as far south as Daytona Beach and I cruised along the beach with my helmet off, enjoying the salty air and feeling like "Easy Rider" with the ocean waves crashing just a few feet from my tires. I discovered the contrasts of travelling alone where you could remain alone or easily meet other people. A simple "hello" or "where are you from?" can start a new friendship in some cases. The time alone on the open road is my quality time where you can easily slip into a state where soul searching can become your favorite pass time.

On my route back home I road up the Florida coast through Georgia, and the Carolinas. I rode through Washington, D.C., just to say I was there. My time and cash supply were limited so I headed west for home. I never really knew what a toll road was and they weren't marked as such on the map back in those days.

The tolls quickly chewed up the remainder of my cash somewhere in the middle of Ohio. I was close enough to home to make it there that same day but my gas tank was empty, I was hungry, and I was out of cash. I swallowed my pride and stopped in at an Ohio State Police station. I explained my dilemma to a State Trooper who took pity on me, and lent me $10 from his own pocket. I had just been hired as a police officer myself and I truly appreciated the professional courtesy, but it was still quite embarrassing.

I filled up my gas tank and settled on a Snickers bar to hold me over until I got closer to, or actually home. I crossed the Ambassador Bridge into Canada having to switch my gas tank over to reserve. I was able to make the toll that was only about 75 cents back then. I made it home with 15 cents in my pocket, an empty gas tank and stomach; but I made it! I learned some valuable lessons on that trip......the most important one of all....that I wanted to do it again!

Coast to Coast

After catching the bug I've continued to explore Canada and the U.S. on two wheels. I've been as far north as Hyder, Alaska, south to Daytona Beach, Florida and from the source of the Mississippi to New Orleans. I did the west coast from San Francisco to Vancouver, then came back home all the way across the Northern States. I rode to the east coast and did the Cabot Trail on Cape Breton Island. I trampled a good path through many of the southern states, in and around the Smokey Mountains, and rode most of the Blue Ridge Parkway. I went as high as the top of "Pikes Peak" in Colorado. I rode through cold, snow capped mountains, across miles of golden wheat fields, through giant redwood forests, and along huge blue oceans.

I remember the days of cheap roadside motels where you could park your bike right at the front door, and gas stations with real attendants who would hand you the nozzle for fear of spilling gas on your shiny bike. More and more I learned to search out the less travelled path, and use the old state highways and scenic byways, unless I really had to make time or be some place. Over the years I noticed the gas stations became scarcer, and motels could only be found near major interchanges with the Interstate highways. Mom and Pop convenience stores and restaurants closed, and were replaced by the large chain operators.

Transforming and Transcendence

The population also shifted from small town America to the larger city centers. On my ride along the Mississippi I could see the transformation or progress of transportation unfold before my eyes. The mighty river was once the only way to penetrate the interior of the country unless you were under horsepower. Along the rivers man then laid the steel ribbon and used the locomotive to carry even more than the mighty riverboats and barges once did. Then the automobile came along, and man built roads where people and products could be moved easily and rapidly. Eventually the Interstate system was built so everything and everyone could reach their destinations in the quickest way possible. Lost forever with these mega roads was the joy of river cruising or the enjoyment of a leisurely drive along a winding road that followed the contours of the river and the land. Businesses, and eventually people, moved to follow the progress and the convenience of living in the thriving cities.

One thing I do give the United States Credit for is the building of "scenic roads," some of which were built simply for the enjoyment of driving, and some of the scenic views they have to offer. These old roads get the blood pumping through my veins, and on occasion, have actually given me goose bumps! Try to picture this: I was riding the edge of a huge storm one day with pitch black, nasty clouds, somewhere along the Kentucky/Georgia border, in the mountains. The sky above looked like it was going to burst open at any minute and the air was still, cool, and crisp.

There was an amazingly calm lake on my left offering up a perfect reflection of the ominous clouds and sky above. Something caught my eye; I looked up to my left and I saw an American bald eagle gliding along, with me under wing. Just me, that eagle, and Mother Nature looking over us. It doesn't get any better than that!!!

Perhaps we need to thank God for some of the natural pleasures that have been left on this earth for our viewing pleasure. I guess man is responsible too in some ways, since many back roads are still being maintained for our driving and riding pleasure. It is too sad and too bad though, that the small town America that could once be found all along these byways has all but dried up. None the less, my wanderlust and sense of adventure still consumes me and keeps my appetite wet for whatever lies around the next corner of the road. The open road awaits all of us.

"People come and go, but for now they still need roads to get where they're going."

Coco

Puerto Vallarta, Mexico

"Most of my treasured memories of travel
are recollections of sitting."
— *Robert Thomas Allen*

I hadn't been in Mexico a week but I quickly and easily became a regular at a few local watering holes. This is not because I was boozing all the time, but that I find these places are melting pots where all sorts of people and their particular lives unfold right in front of you, if you watch them closely. People from the northern hemisphere make their exodus south in the winter to places like Puerto Vallarta, in Mexico.

One of the local watering holes I grew attached to was "Sweeney's," in the heart of the old downtown Vallarta, only a couple blocks from the beach. In my case it was in a perfect location for a pit stop on the way home from the beach, when the sun had left me parched and in need of hydration. You could always count on the same bar staff, and some regulars for company if you felt like chatting.

When I'm travelling and meeting new people I like to combine a persons name with their hometown, so I can remember them easier. At Sweeney's I met the barmaid Lee Anna from Virginia, Regina Dan and Regina Randy, Tex, Nebraska Archie, and Coco. Nobody is really sure where Coco is from or if that's even his real name. I was travelling solo on this particular trip so I perched myself at the bar with these regulars chatting about how to solve all the world's problems. You always seem to come up with better ideas when relaxing, and drinking a cold beer.

One of the things I love about travelling is the sport of "people watching." In my opinion, everyone is a character and they all have their own story. Some people love to share their life story, and some keep theirs a secret or simply just don't care to share it with anyone. Coco was one of those characters who kept to himself and easily caught my interest. He was a regular at the bar who everyone called by name, kind of like "Norm" from "Cheers." He even had his own spot up against the wall, at a table near the bar. He would just stroll in somewhere around dinner time, take his spot, and either watch the rest of us, or sometimes nod off.

Curiosity got the best of me and I asked some of the regulars what Coco's story was. The story varied, but the consensus was that Coco was homeless; Sweeney's was a safe refuge where he could just come and hang out. He didn't necessarily look homeless, but he was elderly and somewhat weathered, with short hair and a fairly trim build. His eyes were starting to get that glazed look that comes with age, or the onset of cataracts. I could only wonder what those eyes had seen; Coco contently kept to himself. I said hello in Spanish and English a couple times as I walked past him on the way to the washroom, but my presence was barely acknowledged.

Lee Anna says she had no problem with Coco hanging out since he kept to himself, and he didn't bother anyone. I saw her give him water once, but I can't recall ever seeing him drinking any booze. She said he has even left with some of her late night, drunken patrons, walking them safely home. Lee Anna and Nebraska Archie blew me away when they said Coco had walked them home, and they offered him a place to crash. They said when they got up in the morning, Coco would be gone. Archie says he'd seen Coco come and go for at least the ten years he'd been visiting Vallarta.

On one particular night after leaving the bar I had the midnight munchies and I went in search of a snack. I bumped into Nebraska Archie *(seemed to bump into him everywhere, but it is a small town)* at a local taco stand, kind of like the late night drive thru at "Taco Bell," but here you walk up to the window, and you can sit on the patio. While Archie and I were eating we noticed Coco on the sidewalk across the street. Archie called out to him, but he was oblivious to us with the traffic and street noise. I whistled, and Coco came trotting across the street.

Coco joined us on the patio, and the usual nods of acknowledgement were made. I don't usually give street beggars a second glance, but this was Coco and I asked if he was hungry. He just looked at me with those sad brown eyes. I had more food than I needed, so I took one of my tacos and threw it on to the sidewalk near Coco. No, I wasn't being rude, or ignorant in any way; Coco is a dog, a Doberman Pincer to be exact.

"I've met many characters, but new friends come in all forms."

The Fugitive

Puerto Vallarta, Mexico

A good holiday is one spent among people whose notions of time are vaguer than yours.

- J. B. Priestley

I had been in Puerto Vallarta, Mexico for two weeks; now I could add my brother Bernie, and brother in law Larry, to the mix of characters I had met in town at Sweeney's Bar: Virginia Lee Anna, Regina Dan, and Randy, Nebraska Archie, Tex, Just John, Texas Christina, Sarnia Isabella, Esmeralda, César, Roger, and of course, Coco. I've came to learn from my own observations, and with the added comment from Tex, "everyone in Puerto Vallarta has a story, or is there hiding from it."

In general, I found the folks in Puerto Vallarta to be friendly; I was welcomed as a temporary resident, a Snowbird perhaps. I was happy to be accepted as a regular at Sweeney's, but was a little concerned when I heard that I had been spending time in the bar, hanging out with a fugitive. The bar was just buzzing the one day; from what I could gather the local authorities had captured one of the Sweeney's regulars, but he managed to escape shortly after, a feat that is apparently not unusual for this character.

I was a little put out that I had not been previously informed of the infamous background of this fugitive, but some of the folks at Sweeney's knew of my previous life as a cop. Perhaps there was a bit of a trust issue. They did tell me that the fugitive was wanted by the authorities, but he finds it easy to hide in plain sight within the throngs of tourists' downtown. Apparently the fugitive was nabbed right in front of Sweeney's and it caused quite a commotion; nobody there likes the authorities, they are known for their brutality and corruption. Somehow, after being captured, the fugitive managed to escape during the commotion; probably a distraction technique used by the locals.

I must say I was more than a little curious about the whole event, and I wondered if we really know just who anyone really is anymore. I just had to know who this criminal mastermind was, since he obviously was aware of whom I was. Well you know how it is; just when you think you've heard it all, someone pointed out you know who to me...Coco! Oh my God, how could this be? Not our sweet and innocent Coco? We all know how cruel life can be; Coco was unlicensed, homeless, and as it turns out, "on the lam" for most of his life. Coco was a street smart hound who had somehow managed to avoid capture, sometimes aided by the locals, who would let him hide out, kind of like the "James Gang" of the old west. It would seem that he has even perfected the art of escape, going along with his capture, only to escape when the authorities turn their backs *(apparently he knows how to slip out of his noose)*.

You can call me a softy, but even though Coco is a fugitive I really didn't mind having him watching my back from his usual spot against the back wall. He looked pretty tuckered out that day, so I placed the pork chop bone from my dinner under his nose as a peace offering. He accepted my gift, and then chewed on it as I went back to socializing. A short time later I felt something brush against my leg; I looked down from my bar stool to see Coco. He was just sitting there quietly; he never bothered anyone when they had food on their tables. I bent over and put my hand out to give him a pat on the head; to my astonishment Coco raised his right paw for a hand shake...Oh My God...How Cool Was That?

"We love you Coco!!!"

The Walkabout

Phnom Penh, Cambodia

"One always begins to forgive a place as soon as it's left behind."
– Charles Dickens

I had been a public servant for over 31 years; survived being a city cop, and now I was retired! I had discovered over the years that I loved to travel, see strange new places, and experience new things, in different countries. I had also "vacationed," taking in dozens of destinations, mostly all-inclusive resorts. I always got the itch to wander and see what lay beyond those tall fences. My buddy Michael, who moved to Southeast Asia years earlier, suggested I should come and visit there some day. Since I now had the time to explore strange new places, I decided to take Michael up on his offer. I saw many, many weird things in my policing career but you know what they say? "You ain't seen anything yet."

The flights to the other side of the globe were grueling, and the longest stretch of time I had ever spent off the ground. I flew from Detroit to Tokyo, and then to Bangkok; about 21 hours in the air. I'm not into huge, dirty, noisy cities like Bangkok, and maybe I was just a bit intimidated by it, so I decided to rest up in an airport hotel outside the city, and jump on another plane to Phnom Penh, Cambodia the next day. A nice leisurely day hanging around the pool seemed better than anything I could imagine in Sin City *(Bangkok)*. Michael had to work for a living and wasn't going to be able to meet me until the afternoon, so my later flight would work out just fine and I could start on my tan. Michael teaches English in Phnom Penh to support his own habits of wanderlust.

I felt like a V.I.P. upon arrival at the Phnom Penh Airport; Michael had a taxi driver waiting for me, holding a sign with my name on it. The ride to my hotel was shorter than I expected. I took special notice of the lack of rules on the road; there were no traffic lights, or stop signs. The traffic seemed to be flowing though, kinda like syrup running all over your pancakes; it's flowing, but where is it going? The biggest vehicles earned the right of way, and pedestrians took their life in their hands as they dodged the hordes of honking scooters. It was not unusual to see 3 or 4 people on these little motorcycles; men, women, children, and none with helmets. I witnessed this organized chaos first hand; I survived it, and was promptly delivered to my hotel that Michael had pre-arranged.

On my arrival at my hotel, "The Walkabout," Michael was perched at the bar, with a cold beer waiting. He told me the place was all mine for 15 bucks a night. I took a quick peak at my room while I dumped my luggage, it appeared adequate; clean, a shower, and air conditioning. That was just fine; my beer was getting warm. Michael had gotten a head start on me, but I gave it my best to catch up. I didn't pay much attention to the girl that had moved over to let me sit on the bar stool beside Michael until I felt a hand on the inside of my thigh. Now, I hadn't seen Michael in a few years prior to this visit, but we never had that kind of a relationship. To the best of my knowledge things had not changed. Mike saw me looking down into my lap and he just smiled, it was not his hand, but the gal's beside me.

I half-heartedly assumed the gal was just being friendly with the strange new white guy; Michael said something to her and she left. I was more interested in catching up with Michael and my beer. As I got a little more hydrated and comfy in my surroundings, I noticed there were about 15 Asian women in the bar, and many of them were checking me out. They all seemed very friendly, some were playing pool and some were just hanging out at the bar. I just had to ask, Michael explained it like this: he said, "Any gals behind the bar work for the bar, and any gals on our side of the bar are working us."Ohhh, yeah, Welcome to Cambodia!

Michael thought I should sample some real Cambodian food and the local fare. We went to a nearby restaurant for dinner where we were the only two white people there. Michael was somewhat aware of the Khmer customs and he did the ordering for us. I was willing to try anything since I'm not a fussy eater, but have to admit I'm a wimp when it comes to hot spicy stuff. We thoroughly enjoyed the quail, squid, and Riblets, 2 orders of fried rice with crab, prawns, and 2 pitchers of beer. The bill was only $18! It definitely paid to eat where the locals did. One thing I quickly came to hate in Cambodia were the tiny, thin paper napkins they give you, about the same as one single sheet of toilet paper (*even more hilarious was the brand name "Doo-Doo" on the box*). It was quite obvious that everyone there felt the same; apparently it was customary to throw your used napkins, and some food scraps on the floor beside your table. This wouldn't have been so bad if someone was there cleaning it up, but that didn't take place until the end of the night. I guess it is best to dine early if that sort of thing bothers you.

Michael knew all the right places to get the cheapest beer after dinner, but we eventually headed back to "The Walkabout" since it was on his way home, and my place to bed down for the night. The night had brought in a new group of working girls but they looked exactly the same as the day time gals. Like in any other occupation, there are the good, the bad, and the ugly! A couple of the girls were obviously on the "Jenny Crack Diet," or working to support some type of drug habit; it's the same all over the world. I watched, and saw some of the girls disappear up the back stairs with male bar patrons.

I've worked in Morality *(Vice)* and I've had drug informants who were prostitutes, so I am no stranger to how the business works. I was to learn one more lesson though there in Southeast

Asia; I found out that you could rent the girls and a room by the
hour. You just went to the bar with the girl, and they gave you a
room key for 4 bucks. Condoms were extra. The girls had to show
or leave an I.D. card in the case they robbed, or killed you.
Michael just kept smiling and chuckling, as the new kid on the
block had his training wheels removed. It was great that he was
helping me acclimatize to life in S/E Asia, but he had me staying in
a whore house for shit's sake!

You really have to watch out when you're having fun at a place
like "The Walkabout;" there are no clocks in view, and they are
open 24/7, just like the casinos in Vegas. If my first day in country
was to set the tone for the rest of my trip, it was going to be very
interesting indeed!

"Cheers to Uncle Mikey and the Walkabout!"

A Sensual Awakening

Tonle Sap Lake near Siem Reap, Cambodia

Wandering re-establishes the original harmony which once existed between man and the universe"
— *Anatole France*

I heard the faint chirping of the alarm on my phone as I awoke,
I saw the bright orange sun shining through my curtains,
I smelled breakfast cooking, and drifting up from downstairs.

I hear the rhythmic putt-putt of my tuk-tuk as we motor along,
I see the hustle of people and scooters in the early morning traffic,
I can still smell breakfast in the air.

I hear the loud groaning of road construction machinery,
I see the workers are all covered in long sleeves, scarves and hats,
I can smell a mixture of dust and diesel fumes.

I can hear the city noises fade as I head out,
I start to see some greenery and open spaces,
I can smell my sunscreen lotion; I've just wiped my face.

I hear some loud banging and a whining noise,
I see a local iron worker in his shop; sparks are flying out the door,
I can smell the burning metal.

I hear a rooster crowing,
I see him chasing some baby chicks under a shack in the village,
I smell only the fresh country air.

I hear a lone child giggling,
I see a naked little boy, waving to me from the edge of the road,
I smell the dirty river that flows along side the road.

I hear the sound of sloshing water from the lazy river,
I see water buffalo lounging in the rice fields,
I smell some kind of flower in the air.

I hear the sound of young voices singing,
I see a brightly colored school house, full of children,
I smell the exhaust from the big bus that just passed by.

I hear the sound of loud motors revving in the distance,
I see a hoard of pastel colored, wooden boats in the river,
I smell the smoke from my guide's cigarette.

I hear a dog barking while I'm cruising on the lake,
I see that it lives on one of the little floating houses,
I smell the fishy water all around me.

I hear annoying noise coming from a loud speaker,
I see it's emanating from a floating church, with people at prayer,
I smell wood burning in someone's stove.

I hear the sounds of people, animals, and vehicles,
I see how content the locals around me really are,
I can't smell anything beyond my huge smile.

*"It's the simple things that we sense all around us that make
our travels memorable."*

Bullets, Bugs, and Birds

Siem Reap, Cambodia

"I haven't been everywhere, but it's on my list."
– Susan Sontag

Buses and Crickets

I hadn't been in country *(Cambodia)* a week yet, but it seemed much longer. Perhaps it was the time change, or the 23 hours on airplanes, or exploring the night life in Phnom Penh with my ex-pat buddy, Michael. Somehow the nights turn into days, when there are no clocks, or closing times in many of the city's watering holes. Michael can sniff out a watering hole like a horse dying of thirst in the middle of the desert. His vast knowledge of beer, broads, and brothels helped me acclimatize to my strange and new surroundings in Southeast Asia.

Michael does have a job, and since he had to work I ventured off on my first solo Cambodian adventure. I wanted to see the largest religious ruins site in the world, "Angkor Wat." For those who are geographically challenged or who just don't care about anything in Cambodia, this was the setting for the movie "Laura Croft - Tomb Raider." It was a boring six hours bus ride to Siem Reap, a small city outside of the ruins where you have to stay if you want to sleep and eat in doors. I had purchased a pirated "Batman" DVD that the bus driver was more than happy to play during the long ride. It (*and I*) was a hit with the other passengers. The bus ride was $11, including bottled water and breakfast. I let them play "Batman" for free.

Besides my 2 buck purchase of the DVD, I had nibbled on some local delicacies while wandering and stretching my legs. The tour bus gal was feeding some of the local kids; she offered me a

19

fried cricket from a bag she was eating out of. Now normally, any sane person would not even think about it, but I have to admit I was curious; the locals popped these into their mouths like we do with popcorn at the movies. I also figured a cricket was nothing compared to the farewell lunch I had with Michael the previous day where we shared a Tarantula appetizer. Of course the spiders were deep fried, with a nice Lime dipping sauce! I poked back the cricket not thinking much of it, till one of the legs got stuck in my teeth. The tour gal chuckled; I guess you're supposed to pull the legs off first. I thought it made a great tooth pick! I followed it up with a fresh banana; just in the case my stomach didn't appreciate my sense of adventure in cuisine.

Tomb Raider

I found a room in Siem Reap for 15 bucks a night. I thought the place must have been safe; there was a Sign posted in my hall with pictures of prohibited items that included guns, grenades, and needles. The room seemed descent enough except for the feathers I saw in the shower on the floor; seems a bird was nesting in the exhaust fan so I figured turning it on was not an option. There was no discount for sharing the room. I found that there was also some pretty descent normal food to be had when I checked out a pizza place a few doors down from my hotel. A diet coke was a buck and a half, and a beer was a buck, so I knew I wouldn't be losing any weight on this trip. For the most part, I found Cambodia very cheap. My four night stay at "The Walkabout" including many drinks, and a few meals, was a scandalous $157. You can't stay a single night in a hotel in any major city in North America for that kind of money. In comparison, Michael was paying $160 "per month," plus utilities for his one bedroom apartment.

The city of Siem Reap was really nothing to speak of, but it was the widely accepted jump off point for touring the ruin sites in the area, as well as Tonle Sap Lake with its floating villages. Angelina Jolie took a liking to the city while she was there filming Tomb Raider. I heard she was very generous to the poor locals, and that she and the film crew hung out at a place called the Red Piano. I made a pit stop there and took note of all the pictures of her on one wall, near her favorite booth. I'm sure if you paid enough you could even sniff the seat she sat in. On a positive note the movie star and the popularity of the movie were a boon for the café and the city.

When you travel on your own it always pays to make new contacts and use any that you already have. When I was in Phnom Penh Michael introduced me to a guy who gave me the name of a reputable guide in Siem Reap. I had made arrangements to meet the guide ahead of time and it paid off. He was waiting at the bus stop in the middle of nowhere with my tuk-tuk and driver. How could I even question the hefty $15 "per day" taxi, and the extra expense of the guide at $20 per day? Hell, I could spend that at one sitting with a decent meal and a few drinks! I have found in my past experience that viewing ruins *(sometimes just piles of rock)* without a knowledgeable guide is just like looking at "a pile of rocks."

I liked the guide immediately when he suggested using a back entrance to the ruins to avoid the large crowds, and to beat the afternoon heat. The ruins of Angkor Wat cover something like 12 square kilometers, so I chose to do a two day tour that only covered a few of the most prestigious ruin sites. These ruins date back to the 7th century when the Khmer Rulers continually tried to out do each other by building bigger and better temples. The Hindu, and later Buddhists carved out their history on the facades of these elaborate temples. The different sites vary in style, and in their state of condition or restoration. The temples were swallowed by the jungle many years ago, before any attempt at preserving or restoring them was taken on. I could not do the ruins justice by trying to describe the different colors, textures, and carved stone structures. It is one of those places you just have to see to get a true appreciation, and comprehension of it.

Floaters

Another day trip for me from Siem Reap was a ride out to Tonle Sap Lake to see the floating villages. My morning ride to the lake was a sensual journey in itself; it inspired another story, or poem of sorts (*A Sensual Awakening*). My tuk-tuk guy took me right to a boat guy; they all have cousins or connections in the tourist trade. My boat guide was a cool, good looking Asian kid with a haircut as fancy as his shiny cell phone. He helped me climb aboard, and then he sat back in his plastic lawn chair and fired up a smoke. The tour was mostly "seeing as you go" with no narration; not that it would have even been possible to hear anything over the roar of the viciously loud motors on the rickety wooden boat. Getting out of the bay was quite chaotic with wood boats of all sorts and sizes jockeying for position, the bigger ones getting the right of way.

The water was muddy; it was the color of chocolate milk, but the fishy smell set you straight. The wooden boats were all painted different colors with huge exposed, screaming motors. Once we got out of the bay it got a little quieter and I started to appreciate the uniqueness of this place. Other boats were docked or tied up to multi-colored wooden homes built on rafts, anchored, and floating on the lake. I saw wood stoves burning, women doing laundry, dogs lounging, and children playing; all on, or in their floating world. Keep in mind there would be no fresh water or electricity, or plumbing in these places. So, where I saw the one woman doing her laundry, her neighbor could have just dumped the family sewage. I could only imagine where the dog did its business.

I cruised by a school gymnasium, pool hall, church, variety store, and a bar; all neatly built on rafts, and floating on the lake. I was told one of the reasons people gravitate to these villages is that they cannot be taxed; they are not "on anyone's property." They are like Gypsies on water. I saw a couple houses on the move; I figured they just decided they didn't like the neighborhood anymore, or wanted to change the view. My guide stopped at a huge barge where there was a restaurant, museum, and a cage of baby Crocodiles; anything can be bought, or sold in Cambodia. I was amazed at the peace and tranquility of the village as a whole. I could only stare as a young girl paddled by me, balancing herself on the bow of her carved, wooden canoe. Her innocent smile said it all, "Life is good!"

The Kalashnikov

I've always been intrigued by war, and the multitude of stories of heroism and horror that go along with it. I have learned a lot in the past about the Viet Nam War, but I was only vaguely aware of what "The Killing Fields" in Cambodia were really all about. A short self guided tour there was enough to seriously depress any person with a conscious, and I think it is really beyond anyone's comprehension as to what actually took place there. In a nut shell, it was after the war, in 1979, when the Khmer Rouge systematically massacred two or three million (*exact numbers are unknown*) of there own people who didn't share the same political views.

"The Killing Fields" is an actual place out in the middle of nowhere, where people were taken by the truck load to be slaughtered, and buried in mass graves; men, women, and children! The soldier executioners found that ammunition was too expensive to waste on these people so they used machetes, axes, shovels, hoes, and even rakes to butcher them. Only some of the mass graves have been excavated, revealing piles of the severed limbs and skulls of people who will never be identified. A huge glass pavilion stacked with human skulls serves as a monument to the atrocity. The end result of this mass genocide is that 80 % of the Country's remaining population is under the age of 30 years. It also sent the country back into the dark ages; most doctors, lawyers, engineers, teachers, etc were eliminated from existence.

My next stop was suggested by my tuk-tuk driver, and although I thought it was completely freakish considering what I had just seen, I once again decided to expand my horizons. We stopped at some type of military camp where you can shoot any type of automatic weapon that you want, depending on how much cash (*and ammunition*) you are willing to spend. It seemed the army was a little shy on cash or that these particular guys found a way to make an extra buck. I picked out the infamous "Kalashnikov" or "AK47" assault rifle, the weapon of choice bought from the Russians, by the North Vietnamese. For 50 bucks I got to bang off 40 rounds at a fixed target. Man, did that thing bark!

My guide seemed to take more pleasure than I did in the small fireworks display. He asked if I wanted to try a 20 caliber machine gun, but it wasn't in my budget and I'm not really a gun freak (*I carried a firearm as a Cop for 30 yrs*). My last stop on the way home was at an upscale graveyard with huge and elaborate tomb stones, or monuments. This was apparently the resting place of the rich and famous in the area, unlike those poor souls who were in the mass graves not too far away.

"Just one day in Cambodia makes you truly appreciate the word Freedom really means."

The Hog and the Cow

Phnom Penh to Koh Kong, Cambodia

"We wander for distraction, but we travel for fulfillment."
– Hilarie Belloc

The dusty, red "Harley Davidson Softail Classic" was delivered to me at my hotel, "The Walkabout," while I was staying in Phnom Penh, Cambodia. My friend Michael had previously introduced me to Murray from Australia, who owns a local tour company that rents motorcycles. I had explored this touring option before going to Cambodia, and then discussed it further over a few beers with Aussie Murray, and Michael. Murray agreed to rent me a hawg for three days for $450 U.S., and he would supply a support vehicle to follow me in the case of a break down. Michael and his buddy Colorado Ted decided to be the support team, driving Murray's pick-up truck. Murray was to come along on his own bike to lead the tour.

Aussie Murray took ill and sent his buddy Alaska Mark in his place. Mark apparently knew the route we would be taking and had done the ride before. He was riding a 400cc "Suzuki Intruder." I knew he wouldn't have any problems finding fuel with the abundance of rice in Cambodia (*Japanese bikes are referred to as rice rockets*). Harley's are quite rare anywhere in Asia so the tuk-tuk drivers were in awe when I explained to them how the 1400cc Harley engine was about six times the size of their scooters. I must admit I did have my doubts about taking the bike out into Phnom Penh traffic after witnessing the chaos personally.

No helmet was supplied with the bike, but there was a new helmet law that had just come into effect. I recalled watching the police one day, hiding on the sidewalk and jumping out into traffic to ticket no-helmet offenders on scooters. It was quite comical;

most of the scooters just darted around the police and refused to stop. The cops were quite helpless since they were on foot, and had no vehicles to chase the offenders. I heard the fine was only about 25 cents but who knows what they would do to a "Barang" (*the name they call white foreigners*).

I usually wear a helmet when riding my own motorcycle at home; I thought I should abide by the new law so I went across the street to buy a helmet at some sort of sporting goods store. I managed to find a shiny red helmet to match the bike. It was 12 bucks but I got it for 7 because it was a display model and covered in dust. It looked more like a polo helmet, but it would suffice. Still thinking about the traffic situation, I recalled some advice from another guy I met, an ex-CFL football player named Tim. He said you just pick up a "blocker" and follow them through traffic and uncontrolled intersections. His second piece of advice was to NEVER stop for the Police or at any accident scene where you may be at fault. Apparently if you are white, then YOU are at fault. I did wonder about the accident thing since I signed no contract, or Insurance agreement for the bike rental.

Mark and I mounted up and I let him lead the way through the city traffic, with him being "my blocker." The traffic was definitely organized chaos! It consists mostly of motor scooters that zip in and out and around you from all directions. One of the guys had previously told me there was only one rule that really applied in traffic; "the biggest vehicle has the right of way." The Harley was a big bike in comparison to all the scooters so I did gain some right of way. The loud roar of the exhaust pipes also helped in traffic, turning several heads along the sidewalks. One young gal on the back of a scooter gave me a big smile; I cracked the pipes and I think she wet herself! I must admit I looked pretty cool with the matching helmet, 5 buck Raybans, and my Harley shirt with a picture of a Bulldog wearing an American Flag bandana and the words, "Bad to the Bone."

The first day's ride was to Sihanoukville, about five or six hour's away taking the scenic route. There was a variety of road conditions we had to deal with along with the kids, dogs, chickens, and cows actually "in" the roadway. Passing was a little unnerving as you overtook large trucks; at the same time they were overtaking scooters. There are some painted lines on the roads but I think they are only there for show. There are also some speed signs but I have no idea how the law would be enforced since the cops can't afford radar guns. I realized it was Friday the 13th; a great day to practice riding a strange bike, on dangerous roads, in a foreign country where I couldn't read or speak the language!

The weather was hot and humid as usual, but the air got cooler the faster we went. Mark and I lost Michael and Ted somewhere in traffic; they couldn't pass as easily as we could on the bikes. Mark found, and then pulled into our hotel in Sihanoukville; I'm not sure which was better, the pool or the cold beer!

The next day (*Saturday*) was another of those sensual awakening days. It probably helped that I was refreshed, and not hung over like I was when we left on Friday. The trek took us on hilly and winding roads with some switchbacks, along the coast of the Bay of Thailand. Mark let me take the lead and I got into the groove enjoying that feeling we bikers get when at peace; and one with the open road. I quickly learned to stay sharp in the turns where sand or gravel was sometimes scattered across the road. Then I'd get overconfident on the nice pavement only to lean too hard into a steeply banked turn and bottom out the running boards. That will wake you up in the morning! The road was surrounded on both sides by thick jungle so I got to enjoy some cooler air and very light traffic.

It was a great ride through the mountains, similar to the Smoky Mountains in the U.S. I've been on many roads during my travels and seen many things, but just when you think you've seen it all...you see a sign that says "Elephant Crossing!!!"

27

Unbefreakinglievable, not only did I have to watch for debris, kids, scooters, and farm animals on the road, now I had to watch for elephants! I had to stop and take of picture of this sign so the folks back home would believe me. Mark pulled up to me, smiled, and said, "Welcome to Cambodia."

I didn't get to see any Elephants on the road but the Cow and Water Buffalo traffic was getting pretty thick. I learned as I went along that these critters usually move forward while crossing the road, so it was best to pass behind them. Mostly, they would ignore the sound of your horn, and they crossed at their leisure. I came upon six or seven huge Cows on a bridge up ahead of me on the road. I slowed down to look for an opening or way through them, but this one big bastard thought he owned the whole bridge! I was trying to get behind grandpa but he was still too close, and he ignored my horn. Hmmm, Plan B....I yanked the clutch in and cranked the throttle hard twice letting loose some Harley thunder. Holy Cow! Gramps jumped, and spun around looking like Michael Jackson doing "The Moo Walk." It was hilarious!

I laughed out loud and smiled so hard I could barely see over my moustache! A short time later I came up on a scooter with a Cambodian Monk decked out in his orange robes, riding on the back, side saddle. I needed to pass the scooter; I was having so much fun I just couldn't resist a little more thunder. I've never seen a Monk show any sign of emotion but when I cracked those pipes his eyes popped, his jaw dropped, and he almost fell backwards off the bike. Ah hell, I was just trying to live up to the bad-ass biker image.

The remainder of the ride on Saturday was along the Thailand border, until we reached Koh Kong. We found another gem of a hotel for twelve bucks a night with a welcoming pool. Mark and I got up early Sunday morning, skipping morning mass to beat the heat and get on the road. It was actually a bit cool and foggy in the mountains at that time of the morning, kind of refreshing. My smile quickly found its way back to my face as Mark let me take the lead again to wind our way home. Eventually, the fun stopped as we neared the city and fell victim to the heavy traffic. It can be quite daunting when you see trucks passing each other coming head on at you taking up the whole road. Remember the larger vehicle, right of way thing? You learn to adjust; you just exhale, then pull your left elbow and knee in and ride the right edge of the road. Closing your eyes helps keep the flying dust and debris out of them. Riding on the gravel shoulder is not a good idea.

"Riding in Cambodia was hawg heaven!"

Bus # 94

Phnom Penh, Cambodia

*"The open road is a beckoning, a strangeness,
a place where a man can lose himself."*
— *William Least Heat Moon*

To say Cambodia is an interesting place would be a gross understatement. I could try to describe the many things I did and saw on a daily basis, but in this case I will relate a one day adventure to try and help you see things somewhat from my own perspective. One tidbit of information as an *intro* to this story that is hard to comprehend is that eighty percent of Cambodia's population is under the age of thirty. This was as a result of the genocide imposed by the Khmer Rouge from 1975 to 1979. In some ways I found this accounts for the young, immature, and undereducated service industry that is trying to run the country.

When I first hooked up with my buddy Michael in Cambodia, we shared some beers, and worked on a plan to do some travelling somewhere in the country that he had not been to yet. We decided on the Northeast section of Cambodia, or the Mondulkiri province since Michael had not yet explored that part of the country. Michael acted as our travel agent and bought us each a six dollar bus ticket to Kratie, which was to be our first over night stop on our self guided tour.

The bus was to leave at 8:00 a.m. the next morning so we thought it best to discuss the final details over beers at my hotel, "The Walkabout." Since this bar *(more like a brothel)* has no clocks, and runs 24/7 we didn't realize that our discussion had carried on a wee bit late; we thought that we should get at least four hours sleep before we had to catch the bus. Like the travel trooper he is, Michael met me at 7:15 a.m. sharp at my hotel. He

30

immediately apologized for the excess luggage he had brought; it was about the size of a bowling bag. I knew that I needed something greasy in my stomach to start my day and ordered some kind of bacon and egg sandwich. More the man than I, Michael opted for an icy cold, draught beer.

We caught a tuk-tuk taxi out front to take us to the bus depot (*Michael bartered the guy down to a buck and a half from two, as usual*). The bus was late to arrive at the depot but I learned that this is quite normal in Cambodia, and patience is a virtue, or so they say. Those of us with tickets boarded the bus but it seemed we were not to depart until the seats were all full; something else I learned was the norm. No big deal I thought, since the bus filled quickly. We departed the station only to stop directly across the street at the gas station to fill up. Once again I had to remind myself to relax; they did have to gas up at some point.

While we were getting gas Michael and I noted a commotion at the front of the bus; we had great seats in the front row with extra leg room. There were four guys pointing at, and arguing in Khmer about the gauges on the dashboard, apparently one of them wasn't working. Besides the extra leg room, our front row seats afforded us a great view through the windshield; well, except for the cracks, and the 28 different stickers, and the duct tape patch on the driver's side. I think the duct tape was some sort of sun screen for the driver.

The commotion subsided and one of the guys left the bus. Two of the other men stayed on the bus and the driver took his seat. You could tell he was a professional by the neatly pressed grey slacks, long sleeved blue shirt and black ball cap with gold braiding on the peak; something like a navy ship's admiral would wear. His uniform was complimented by his pink tie that was about a foot too short. I decided to call him "Moe." He put the engine into gear, we lurched forward about two feet, and the bus stalled. Moe calmly tried clutching and shifting gears, only to stall a couple more times. Michael and I just looked at each other and agreed that this was going to be the best six bucks we ever spent!

Moe finally got our Bus running, and in gear; we inched our way into traffic along the streets of Phnom Penh. Moe and the other two guys behind him seemed to be acquainted, or perhaps they worked for the bus company. One of them had a clean white shirt on, and he kind of looked like Antonio Bandarez; I called him "Larry." The third guy had the "Blues Brothers" type of dark sun glasses on *(way cooler than the five buck Raybans I had just bought)*, along with a black straw fedora hat. I called him....yup; you guessed it, "Curly." If you don't get the picture yet, you will as I go on.

Moe maneuvered the big bus through the heavy traffic of Phnom Penh, a feat in itself considering that the heavy traffic does flow, but it is bumper to bumper, and most intersections are not controlled by traffic lights or stop signs. Then you have to take into account the thousands of scooters or small motorcycles that dart in and out of traffic from lane to lane. The only rule I could figure out was that the larger vehicle has the right of way. Pedestrians have no standing, and cross the busy roads at their own risk. I also noted that everyone likes to use their horns A LOT. Michael says it's a right of way thing; you honk your horn as you pass through, or enter an intersection to state your intention. Then, in the case of an accident, they can say they warned you first.

It didn't take me long to regret sitting up front since Moe really liked the air horn and blew it constantly. Maybe I wouldn't have noticed it as much if it weren't for my severe hangover. As I watched the organized confusion, and traffic flow, I heard a loud thump on my side of the bus near the passenger door. I assumed we had hit a scooter, or it had hit us, but the three stooges only glanced over, and then ignored the situation. Not that Larry would have noticed; his cell phone constantly rang out loud. It seems that no one in Cambodia uses the vibrate mode, and to make Larry's

32

calls even more annoying, all his ring tones were "love songs." Curly did nothing but observe his two comrades. I wasn't sure if he was learning how to drive a bus or that maybe he was the head instructor for the Cambodian school of bus driving, and he was grading Moe's performance.

The real fun began a couple or three hours into the trip when the people at the back of the bus started screaming. I could smell something burning, but just assumed it was some of locals I saw burning grass in the fields. Moe brought the bus to a stop on the road completely blocking the entire right lane. You have to understand that no one gives up their part of the road in this country. Everyone shares the road....buses, trucks, cars, scooters, bicycles, pedestrians including toddlers barely old enough to walk, and a variety of large, and small animals. Several vehicles honked at us as they passed and "the boys" went out to investigate. They returned a few minutes later after a thorough inspection, and someone mumbled something about the brakes. No problem, Moe just drove faster to keep the brakes cool. I did find it a little odd how he lollygagged on the open country roads, but then gunned it through the populated villages while blasting the damn air horn. I tried to see how fast we were going but the speedometer was broken.

Moe actually slowed right down in one village where I noticed that a person was laying under a blanket on the side of the road, presumably dead. There was some type of emergency vehicle on hand and they must have been preserving the scene; no one had moved the women's shoes or groceries off the road. Moe just drove right over top of them along with the other traffic. I now understood why he liked his air horn.

Just when things had quieted down and I was nodding off I heard another thud, this time from the windshield. It looked like we hit some kind of bird. Shit does happen, but no....Larry screamed out and Moe jumped on the binders. Maybe I was wrong and we hit another person while my eyes were closed? Larry bailed from the bus and ran off somewhere out of sight; Curly followed shortly after. Being in charge of the bus but not wanting to miss out on anything, Moe decided he would join them. A few minutes later he stooges returned and Larry was holding a dead bird, it looked like a Cockatiel. Ok, maybe it was lunch? Larry proudly displayed the road kill to all the passengers; the old woman across the isle from me grabbed it by the wings and sized it up. I had to assume that maybe she had some expertise in cleaning the fowl. Of course I snapped a picture just to prove this part of the story is not complete bullshit. Larry took the bird back as we got underway again and held it is his lap for awhile; then he displayed it on the dash so Moe could enjoy the sight of his road kill.

I thought we were "almost there" when I heard yet another thumping sound at the front, on my side of the bus. Moe stopped, and the boys went out to investigate again. We were instructed to get off the bus in the middle of nowhere in the ninety degree heat; I saw the right front tire was flat, only on the bottom of course. Michael and I knew this was going to be a major affair for "the boys," so he got out his beer divining rod and steered us to a road side stand within walking distance. He is a master at sniffing out a cold beer and sure enough the little stand had a few on ice for us. There were also lots of snacks on display, but I wasn't hungry enough to try one of the dried Bats, Frogs, or Snakes that were hanging proudly on display in the scorching heat.

The world always seems like such a nicer place from a shady seat with cold beer in hand. Our bus adventure became another travel experience; we sat and watched "the boys" try to flag down passing trucks. It seems they had no tools to fix the flat, *(go figure)*. The woman running the stand took a liking to Michael; he took a liking to the palm wine she offered him. She even called on a single girlfriend to come and meet Michael. I was being educated and amused by the guy out in the field scaling the sugar palm tree like a spider monkey. They tap the trees like we do with Sugar Maples in Canada and make sugar, or wine. Of course we, as Canadians are a little smarter and tap "the bottom" of the trees, saving a lot of climbing.

Our gig was up; a couple other people from the bus wandered over our way to join us for a drink. By now Grandma and all the kids were out checking out the white people; I got in some good photo ops. A few beers for me, a couple of mugs of Palm wine for Michael and "the boys" were waving us back to the bus.....Shit! We boarded the bus with the rest of the passengers who had been standing in the sweltering heat the whole time. I noticed the dead bird while getting back on the bus; it had leaked blood all over the dashboard. Moe got us back underway and we drove for about five minutes until we pulled into Kratie, our final destination. Michael and I just howled since we could have walked that stretch and beaten the bus there; it was now two hours late!

"Hop on the bus Gus."

A Royal Tour

Sen Monoron, Cambodia

*"All the pathos and irony of leaving one's youth behind is thus
implicit in every joyous moment of travel: one knows that the first
joy can never be recovered, and the wise traveler learns not to
repeat successes but tries new places all the time."*

– Paul Fussell

Our bus adventures took us from Phnom Penh to Kratie, and
then on to Sen Monoron in the untamed, northeast section
of Cambodia. The second half of the trip to Sen Monoron was
spent in a beat up bus, on a dirt road for over four hours! If you
ever want to take a trip to "the boonies" this was it. Mikey is a well
seasoned traveler and he promised me a no frills adventure off the
beaten path. Our bus, but not a hotel was booked in advance; once
in Sen Monoron we had to hike up the road towards town in search
of lodgings. It always seems the bus stations are never actually "in
town."

I can't remember if Michael had the hotel on a list or if we just
stumbled across it, but we found a really nice place that just didn't
fit into its neighborhood. It was too nice. Of course we had to pay
top dollar for such a find and since I wanted a hot shower and
private bath we had to pay a whole fifteen bucks each for our
rooms. Michael would normally think paying such a price was
scandalous, but he caved in and enjoyed the plush
accommodations. Actually, I think he was more amused with the
hotel owner Madame Deu. She was a Cambodian woman, fairly
attractive, well dressed, and very outspoken. Her broken English
and Michael's limited Khmer made for interesting conversation.

Madame Deu was immediately taken by Michael's natural
charm. Although there were very few guests staying at the hotel

"in season," the Madame seemed to have enough money to invest in a whole new wing that was in the process of being built. I couldn't really comprehend why, since it was already the largest hotel in town. While I wandered and admired the hotel's finely manicured grounds, gardens, and ample amount of cold beer, Michael hammered out a deal with the Madame for an all day tour up in the surrounding hills, and out in the country. We were in search of the Bousara waterfalls, which we had heard and read about. Jana, a young gal from Prague, was also interested in the tour; the Madame offered us an all day tour for the price of twenty bucks each. Jana was a backpacker who was to be travelling for over a year, and although the price was a bit steep for her taste, she decided she'd join in.

We were all set to head out at around eight in the morning, when Madame Deu said there were some car and driver problems; if we had no objections, she would take us on the tour herself in her brand spanking new Land Rover. With a little arm twisting we accepted the change in plans. We sat and watched as two of the Madame's female hotel cleaning staff loaded up the Land Rover. I'm not sure if it was Michael or myself who had the bigger smile when we saw the case of Anchor beer on ice, getting loaded on board. To my surprise the gals hopped in with us and actually sat in the back with the gear so we paying customers could ride in comfort. It was just as Michael had promised me....a no frills adventure!

We headed out of town and into the mountains; they kind of resembled the Smokey's in the southern U.S.A. Thank God we didn't opt for the rented scooters as originally planned! The roads were either dirt or rock, not gravel, but rock with lots of man eating, sized pot holes. The suspension on the Land Rover definitely got a work out and I sometimes had great difficulty trying not to spill my beer. Yes, breakfast had been consumed so it was ok to start drinking the beer, Michael said so. We bounced around, driving through the mountains for about an hour, and then we stopped at one of the little villages for a Kodak moment. The locals actually live in straw huts in that neck of the woods and one old guy came out for a photo op. Actually, I think he came out to see who the hot white chick (*Jana*) was. Of course he smiled for her photo.

Our next stop was the Bousara waterfalls. The parking lot was just a cleared section in the middle of the forest; you could hear the falls in the distance. There was no paved lot, entrance gate, or admission fee and really, no one around. I assumed all was quiet because it was still early in the morning. We had a bit of a hike on foot along some dirt paths; the two girls acted as porters hauling our gear. I felt a bit guilty and offered to carry the beer. There were concession stands as you would expect with any tourist attraction, but not like these! Fresh Venison jerky (*pretty tasty actually*) hung in the stalls, along with some kind of filleted fish and live Chickens ready to be slaughtered. I sampled the jerky and bought a bag of deep fried banana chips.

As in many third world countries, the whole family is part of any business; cute little munchkins were playing in the dirt in front of the stands with a fresh batch of fury little puppies. I think it was Grandma with the toothless grin, who held the meat cleaver ready to prepare us a freshly slaughtered chicken if we so desired.

We walked another trail that ended at the water falls. We were told the volume of water would be light because of the dry season but I couldn't tell the difference. The Bousara falls consists of two separate falls; the top one a 165 foot drop and the bottom a 300 foot drop. There is a shallow pond about a hundred yards long between the two. The falls and area around it is unspoiled and natural, not like our Niagara Falls. No gates, fences, guard rails, or park rangers. You could walk right into, or swim in the water below the falls with no one to stop you. There were only a handful of other white folks or tourists there and I felt like we had the place all to ourselves. Some geeky guys with a whole bunch of camera equipment kept following me around taking the same shots that I was; turns out they were a film crew from the Ministry of Tourism making an infomercial.

I just cannot sit still when there's a cool new place to explore, so I wandered around the upper falls and pond taking several pictures, and checking things out. I walked right to the edge of the pond where it spills over the rock ledge to the lower level. It was like standing on the roof edge of a 30 storey building with no railing. Someone warned me to be careful since there had already been three deaths there that year. Shit, it was only the beginning of February! Madame Deu pointed out another path, and told me I could follow it to the base of the lower falls. Michael chose to stay with the women and beer, but Jana decided to go exploring with me. One of the porters led us to the jungle path, and then Jana quickly took the lead. I had a hard enough time keeping up to her on the flat ground; then we came to the stairs.

It was a wooden stairway made out of tree branches. Picture a one hundred foot vertical ladder going straight down, with a shaky hand rail on one side. Jana wasted no time in scrambling down the stairs; not to be shown up by the young chick, I started down the stairs trying to fit my size twelve clodhoppers on to the six inch steps. The porter gal just giggled from behind me; she wasn't coming down. My death grip on the rail, and any other tree branch within reach helped me make it to the bottom.

Upon reaching the river at the bottom of the gorge I could hear the roar of the water fall. I cleared the thick jungle and saw where Jana had disappeared to. There she was, standing right at the base of the 300 foot falls with her arms stretched out. She reminded me of the girl on the bow of the Titanic. The mist from the falls blew out from behind, and around her giving the appearance she was suspended in the clouds. I walked closer; I felt how the water cooled the air, like when you open a freezer door. No picture could capture that moment! Jana and I just stood there in awe. We had the whole place, and that moment, all to ourselves. It was magical!

Meanwhile, back up top, Michael and the gals had already gotten into our picnic lunch the Madame had packed for us. They had it all laid out in a nice shady gazebo. Michael handed me a well deserved cold beer; some chuckles from the girls came my way. It would seem that Jana managed to stay completely dry but I was soaked in sweat from head to toe. I inhaled a few coolies to rehydrate and noticed Michael feeding one of the locals. It was the toothless Grandma, another victim of Michael's charm no doubt. The gals had prepared us a delicious curried beef and rice dish. I was the hero when I produced my banana chips for desert.

The film crew couldn't help but admire us good looking tourists and invited us to be in their infomercial. I slipped on my Hollywood shades and we did some posing for them.

From Bousara, we drove awhile and the Madame led us to another smaller waterfall. This place was again unique; the waterfall just appeared from the thick jungle, and it dropped to a small lake. This time we were the only ones there, and we had the whole place all to ourselves! Jana wasted no time; before I even got to the water's edge she had stripped down to her bikini and dived into the lake. Michael and I didn't share her insight and had to improvise by stripping down to our boxer shorts; more giggles from the peanut gallery. By the time we got into the water Jana was standing on the rocks under the waterfall with the water pounding down all around her. She stole the show again when she did a perfect swan dive through the cascading water, and into the lake. Show-off!

Just when we thought the day was done and we were almost home, Madame Deu stopped at a beauty salon owned by her sister. We weren't quite sure what she had in mind there, and I was not looking for a hair cut. Jana chickened out, but Michael and I were troopers and we surrendered. As it turned out we were treated to a deluxe shampoo and scalp massage. It was quite interesting to say the least; I learned all about that fine line between pleasure and pain, when the woman dug her fingers and nails into my head. Jana took pictures, and she was the one doing the giggling.

Sporting our new hairdos, we were treated to one last excursion as the day faded. Then Madame's Son took us up to the top of the highest hill in town, a lover's leap type of overlook, above the town. We stood there soaking up the sunset, panoramic view, and the remainder of the beer. A nice bonfire was waiting for us when we returned to the hotel.

Three and one half years after this adventure Michael came to visit me in Canada. He said he had brought me a special gift and he slid a shiny disc into my DVD player. It was an infomercial from the Cambodian Ministry of Tourism office; and wouldn't you know it, there we were right near the end of the film, posing in front of the water falls at Bousara!

"I am not a celebrity, but I was definitely on a Royal Tour!"

Mad Max and the Mud Road

Mondulkiri Provence, Cambodia

*"Without new experiences, something inside of us sleeps.
The sleeper must awaken."*
                                                    – Frank Herbert

I had thought the bus journey to Sen Monoron, Cambodia was a bit of an adventure, but the real deal was about to come. Michael and I were having a couple of coolies in some little restaurant bar with the only Internet in town, when a guy came wandering in asking if he could still get something to eat. This guy looked like something the cat dragged in. His hair was a mess, his clothes were muddy and wet and he looked like he just ran a marathon through the jungle. He mumbled something to the host that his bus had broken down. The man's remark caught our attention since we were awaiting a confirmation of our bus' departure time in the morning. We had heard that it would be late getting in due to wet weather and bad road conditions.

Once the broken down, weary guy caught his breath, and regained some strength, he told those of us listening that his bus got stuck in the mud about ten miles from town. Apparently the bus got stuck more than once, and the passengers had to push in the pouring rain for over an hour! Eventually the bus got buried too deep and the driver suggested they wait for help to arrive. They were advised against wandering off into the jungle as darkness fell upon them. Some of the passengers decided they could not spend the night on the bus without facilities, food, or water, and they would walk into town. This guy was one of the survivors; the worst part of his story was that we knew it was our bus he was talking about.

Our worst fears were confirmed in the morning by the owner of our hotel, Madame Deu. She said the light rain we experienced the previous day was much heavier on the jungle road, making it a muddy mess. You have to understand that we travelled this road on the way into town, and it was our only way back out. It is completely impassible in the rainy season. The road is a two lane dirt highway that took us four hours to travel on the way in. The dirt is more of red clay; everything I owned was covered in red dust when we arrived in town...and that's from being inside the bus! We already had our tickets and considered staying another day, but we already had plans back in Phnom Penh.

Madame Deu and Mad Max came to our rescue. We waited from 8:00 until 9:30am for the missing bus; the Madame got on the phone barking orders out to someone on the other end. She said she could get us a taxi for $70 for the six hour ride back to Phnom Penh. This seemed like a pretty good bargain when you consider there was no alternative. A Swiss couple in the same predicament sweetened the pot by offering to share the taxi and the cost.

A short time later a guy showed up in a Toyota Camry. It had no four wheel drive; should be interesting I thought. It also meant five of us had to squeeze in a compact car for six hours...I'm glad I was the biggest and called shot-gun. Our driver looked like Chachi from the show Happy Day, except he had a huge, scary mole on his right cheek. It had thick ugly hairs sticking out of it that reminded me of the tarantulas I had eaten in Phnom Penh. Madame Deu gave us a big hug good-bye and we headed off to the mud road.

The first part of the road seemed fine since it had mostly dried up but then drip, drip, drips ...on the windshield. Shit! I said, and I muttered something about the rain. Our driver just smiled since he didn't understand a single word of English. Our first challenge was the thick and deep muddy ruts where other vehicles had been stuck; we were on a steep hill, going up. I looked at the driver as he slammed the Camry into low gear and he gripped the steering wheel. He gunned it through the thick mud sliding sideways into the tracks but at least we were moving. Don't ask me why but Mad Max, the Mel Gibson movie came to mind. Maybe I got the impression that the driver, like Max knew that if you stop, you die! You had to be in the car to appreciate the cheering going on, like we were at the horse races. We cheered for Mad Max and the car because we knew if we got stuck, we'd be pushing.

Max did us proud as we crept over the crest of the hill, and slid on down the other side. I patted the dashboard of the car telling Max I liked his front wheel drive hot rod, and that he was my new hero. Max just smiled again and released his death grip on the steering wheel. The rain let up but I could see more obstacles ahead on the road. I saw a large truck that had slid off the road and it was buried up to its axles. There was a towing cable attached to the front just lying in the mud, where it was abandoned. A little further up the road I saw our bus, buried in the thick red mud and going nowhere!

The road continued to be slippery and slick, and a challenge for Max. Then, for some unseen reason the traffic ahead of us came to a halt, and we were at a standstill. We just sat there waiting and Max didn't seem too concerned. I wasn't as patient and got out for a look. Shit!!! From the crest of the hill I looked down into a big valley where all the rain water had funneled into a small lake at the bottom. Cars and trucks were scattered all over the valley, some slipping backwards, down the hill they were trying to climb. Max joined me for a look, and then got on his cell phone. I thought he was going to tell the Madame we had to turn back, but she promised us he'd get us home; I'm sure he was afraid she'd cut his balls off and fry them up with some bananas, in a nice coconut and curry cream sauce.

We all climbed back on board except for the Swiss couple; they apparently thought it'd be more fun to watch and take pictures. Maybe they were thinking ahead of us, knowing if we got stuck we'd be climbing out into a couple feet of muddy water. Max then wheeled around the stopped vehicles, and headed down into the valley towards the muddy lake at the bottom. Timing was on our side; one of the stuck vehicles was towed and pushed out of our path just in time. Max must have figured speed was the key and he gunned it down the hill. We splashed into the water; I could see Max was running on pure adrenaline. We slid from side to side; the mud and water flew up past my window. Mike and I were both hollering more out of fear than excitement as we cleared the water, and crept up the hill..."Yeah Max, give'r!!!"

Whahooo!!!......we broke the crest of the hill and I calmly called out to the Swiss couple to re-join us. We were cooking now with Mad Max, my new super hero. Then, just as you assume you've got it made....more shit happens! Some other clown had gotten stuck in the mud directly in our path, completely blocking the drivable portion of the road. Max eyed the situation; I asked if he thought he could get around him.....he didn't understand a word I was saying, but I knew he was thinking the same thing. The guys pushing the car waved for us to go around so Max went for it. It looked like we were going to just squeak by, but we started sliding off the road towards a huge boulder that was protruding from the muck. I thought, "this is gonna leave a mark" as we slid into the boulder. Max was not happy, and swore something in Khmer as we were stopped dead in our tracks.

As I wondered whether it was better to get out in my sandals, or bare feet into the thick muck, Max got out for a look. I decided to stay put unless Max ordered me out. He shouted something to the morons who had waved us on, and then got back into the car. Max gave me one of those Clint Eastwood type stares, cut the wheel hard, and gunned the engine. We slid off the rock and started to get around the stuck car, when the morons decided to reverse it. We missed the rear bumper by a pubic hair and Max was once again our hero. Three cheers for Mad Max!

For the rest of the trip on the mud road Max just kept his left turn signal on, and honked the horn while passing everything in sight. Once we hit pavement in the next town we stopped for food and gas. Max had some kid wash down his chariot; I had forgotten what color it was with the red slimy covering. Max got us home two hours sooner than the scheduled bus ride, although there was no way the bus would have made it; and this was the dry season!

"Long live Mad Max!"

Universal Language

"Too often travel, instead of broadening the mind,
merely lengthens the conversation."
– Elizabeth Drew

Y ou can go any place in the world, and get just about
anything you need, with the use of only one word. It is a
simple word; it can be used to find you food, water, shelter,
directions, transportation, and even companionship.

"*Hello*" is commonly used as a greeting, even in different
languages.

I've heard people in foreign countries answer their phones in
English, with "*Hello.*"

Saying "*Hello*" at the airport ticket counter means, can I have a
seat on the plane please?

"*Hello*" at the Customs booth, means please do not search my body
cavities.

Hearing the stewardess say "*Hello*" on the plane means buckle
your seat belt please.

Saying "*Hello*" while wandering the airport, means you're lost and
need directions.

Getting a "*Hello*" from a waiting taxi driver means you're about to
get fleeced.

You shout "*Hello*" to the idiot who just cut off your taxi.

You say *"Hello"* to the hotel clerk when you want the cheapest room available.

Hearing *"Hello"* from the street vendors means they want to sell you something.

"Hello" from small children, means they're laughing at the silly looking tourist.

"Hello" from a total stranger on the street, means you're in a small town.

Saying *"Hello"* to a bartender, means you want a cold one pronto.

Hearing *"Hello"* outside a restaurant, means they want you to eat there.

Saying *"Hello"* to the waitress, means you can't read or speak the language and need help.

A" *Hello"* to fellow travelers is a way to make new friends, and to compare travel tales.

Saying *"Hello"* to anyone, will inevitably lead to saying *"Goodbye!"*

Circus City

Pataya Beach, Thailand

"I love to travel, but hate to arrive."
                                    – Albert Einstein

The City

Some folks call Pataya Beach "Sin City" or "The New Bangkok." I personally thought of it as some kind of elaborate circus, with mind boggling entertainment of every kind you can imagine, and some you just can't. Pataya Beach is on the Gulf of Thailand in the southern end of the country. I was told by my buddy Michael in Cambodia that I should check out Pataya, if I was not going to visit Bangkok. His buddy Colorado Ted was a frequent visitor there, and recommended a few hotels in a good area near the beach. I had never even heard of the city before, but it looked like it would work as a base for me to see some of the other parts of Thailand I was interested in.

At first glance, this place could have passed for Miami in the old days, with a busy road that followed miles of sandy beach. On the opposite side of the road were hotels, shopping centers, restaurants, souvenir shops, and the other touristy crap. I walked along the boardwalk that parallels the beach to check things out. First off, I noticed the heat and humidity; I am prone to melting in tropical heat. The shade of the palm trees, and a light breeze off the bay seemed to help a bit. Buying a cheap sweat towel to carry helped me even more. The mile long boardwalk was paved, and it weaved in and out of the trees, facilitating fellow strollers, runners, hookers, and assorted other street vendors. Yes, in Pataya you can even shop for sex during the day, while at the beach.

The traffic on the multi-lane road was thick but fast moving. I noticed a lot of pick-up truck type vehicles with a roof on the back, and people sitting inside. These are called "Bhat Buses," the Bhat being the Thai currency. I think it was about 10 cents to jump on these mini buses; you flagged them down at the curb. You then just hollered or waved at the driver or his helper, when you wanted to get off. Hopefully they would stop long enough for you to safely disembark. Upon looking at the various businesses along the road, I noted familiar names like Burger King, McDonalds, KFC, and even 7-11. The buildings were a mix of architectural styles, and nothing really matched or blended together.

The Beach

The beach seemed to go on in either direction forever with lots of room for every kind of activity (*I believe it's a mile long like the boardwalk*). I saw several jet skis zooming in and out of various sizes of pleasure craft, and some huge multi-level, party barges anchored out in the bay. Between the hordes of boats in the water and throngs of people on the beach, it kind of looked like Normandy on D-Day, but without the bombs and bullets. Out and above the bay, I counted 12 Para sails in one big circle, like airplanes waiting their turn to land. There were countless beach chairs, umbrellas, and huts to be rented. Vendors selling everything from fresh fruit, to shrimp, to knock off sun glasses, wandered from chair to chair, like mosquitoes hunting their next victim.

The People

For the most part, I think the number of tourists in comparison to locals in Pataya is about the same if you include the vendors. I noticed that there were a lot of ex-pats who have retired there, or at least spend a half a year there. There were folks from every corner of the globe, but it became very apparent to me that a majority of the tourists were Caucasian, middle aged men. In most cases they were accompanied by younger Asian women, some with babies. I found the Thai people vane; they were very concerned about their appearance, and yours. They were quick to point out your fat belly, or lack of hair. The guys were always combing or fussing with their hair. The women would not expose any part of themselves on the beach; they'd just roll up their pant legs to wade in the water. They'd cover their mouths while using a tooth pick, but openly pick their noses in public. For the most part, the locals were very friendly....usually because they were trying to sell you something.

Walking Street

Watching the transformation of Pataya from day to night is like watching an empty sky just before a fireworks display. The packed beaches become deserted, and the throngs of people move to the streets, restaurants and abundance of bars. A section of the main road running along the beach shuts down to vehicular traffic at night, and becomes what I could only describe as the wildest carnival I have ever seen! There are gates at either end of this road; it's called "Walking Street." Somehow, the quiet little shops I saw during the day turned into open patios or bars; no walls or doors, just dozens and dozens of small bars, each blaring their own type of music. The neon signs, and bar names varied as differently, as the music and bar patrons. Each bar also had a posse of hostess girls in matching attire; they were posted out front to lure you into their particular watering holes.

I stopped in amazement, gawking at a Go-Go bar where there was an elevated platform over top the open bar; girls in bikini's were dancing and waving you up. For the fancier clubs, there were dark curtains at the street concealing escalators that would whisk you up to the "Ballet Bars." Everything you can imagine is for sale on the street from meat on a stick, to steak and lobster. Everything else is for sale behind the closed doors! There are side streets running off Walking Street, one in particular called "Boys town." Colorado Ted, who I was with at the time chuckled, and then explained to me how it really was a "Boys" street, with many "Lady Boys" or other gay men, in various states of conversion? I later attended a night club show where all the beautiful looking women were actually men, you truly could not tell the difference in many cases; yes, I was sober.

Music or Mime

I wandered into Walking Street one night around 8ish, as it was just winding up. My attention was drawn to the music of Pat Benetar coming from one of the cubicle bars along the street. It sounded good enough for me to stop and grab a beer; I sat down and caught the band playing Highway Star from Deep Purple next. I thought I was back in high school for a minute, and had to wonder if L.S.D. was back in fashion there too. Across the street there was a female Mime wearing a French Maid's outfit, and she was moving to some sort of techno music.

While I was watching the French Maid Mime, a Thai guy in a Black Bart cowboy hat set up a table right in front of me. I thought he was just another vendor about to put his wares on display, but he had a little girl about 6 years old with him. She was dressed in a shiny pink sequin dress. Pedestrian traffic made their way around the table, as the various types of music blared from all around me. The little girl then mounted the table and started doing some type of contortionist act, like you'd see in Cirque du Soleil. The Mime continued to perform, and the roof top dancing girls carried on behind her. It was like being a kid, lying back on the grass on a sunny summer day, while you stared through a kaleidoscope.

Later, I worked my way through the corral of bars to find a bathroom, and I stumbled across a Blues Bar. The band was finishing up "San Francisco," and then I was blown away by their rendition of "Tobacco Road." The female vocalist was attractive and looked Thai, but she didn't sound like it. Her voice was a combination of Janice Joplin, Aretha Franklin, and Louie Armstrong. The lead guitar and sax player were kickin out the jams for sure!

Behind Closed Doors

I'm sure most people have heard sordid stories of places like Thailand, where the sex trade is just another business. You can't walk a hundred feet during the day or night, without someone trying to wave you into a massage parlor of some sort. There is the legit kind; on one occasion I was treated to a full body massage where they do actually walk on your back. There are also places for great foot massages, where I took advantage of a pedicure, beard and nose hair trim, all for about 3 bucks.

There are also the massage parlors that promise you "a happy ending," and one place advertising "happy hour." The two giggling girls out front told me it meant you got 4 hands for the price of 2. I hooked up with some ex-pats one night in their favorite strip bar and witnessed first hand, things I'd only seen in video pornography. Naked women with various sex toys played on elevated platforms, and others danced on the stage. As with many of the bars there, if you see a woman you want, you pay the manager a "Bar Fine;" it gives you exclusive rights to make your own private deal with her. We call that prostitution here at home.

Just when you think you've seen it all, you see something that reminds you that we are all a bit naïve in some ways. I asked an acquaintance of mine who will remain unnamed; to show me something I'd never seen before. He took me to a place called

"Golden Girls" that looked like any other bar on the strip, with young hostesses out front trying to wave you in. My friend had obviously been there before since one of the girls smiled and grabbed him by the arm, ushering him into the bar. I followed and two cold beers were served up pronto. The bar maid babbled some broken English to me asking the usual, "Whey you from?"

My friend disappeared from sight before I knew it; when I asked the girl where he went, she just waived me upstairs. Curiously, I followed her up to another bar. This one was very dark, and there was porn playing on the TV's behind the bar. Another cold beer was set up for me and I saw my friend a few stools down; I barely recognized him in the dim light. Past him, in the corner I saw I guy seated in a big basket chair with some girl's head face first, in his lap. This was no lap dance! I looked back to my friend and asked him where his female friend was; he pointed down under the bar. Yessiree, the bottom section of the bar was actually a curtain that opens up for the girls; they perch themselves on little "milking stools" behind the bar to do the deed. Unbefreakinglievable! A "Blowjob Bar."

"Money really can buy anything in Thailand."

Eddie Murphy and the Golden Girls

Kananchuburi Provence, Thailand

"Let our lessons come from the journey, not the destination"
- Don Williams Jr.

I booked a no brainer trip from Pataya Beach to the Kananchuburi province, in Thailand near the Burma border. This is home to the "Bridge on the River Kwai," that was made famous by the movie of the same name. For those who are unaware this is where the Japanese used allied prisoners from the Second World War to build a railway bridge over the river, and a mountain pass into Burma.

The shuttle bus picked me up at my hotel at 5:30 a.m. sharp! A despicable time of the day in my opinion; the birds were not even up yet, and there were still a couple people drinking at the bar across the street...not unusual in Pataya. I had behaved the previous evening, opting for a movie at the local cinema instead of being one of those people at the bar. I climbed into the van and noted with my one open eye that there were others on the bus; three older black women had the best seats. I wedged myself in and didn't pay the driver much attention, until he managed to get lost only two blocks from my hotel. He was looking for a certain hotel and two missing people, who he assumed had cancelled...probably the ones I had seen at the bar. I thought this was a blessing in disguise; I had learned that no vehicle goes anywhere in Asia unless every seat in the vehicle is full. Now I could try to stretch out a bit.

We headed out of the neon and into the night. My open eye was starting to close, catching up with the other napping one, so I leaned back in my seat to stretch out. Whoa! My seat flew straight back crashing into the guy behind me who hollered something in

German, I think. I was sitting on a fold down, or jump seat that was obviously broken. Oh boy, this was going to be a fun three hour ride! I was fiddling with my seat when the driver flicked on the interior lights welcoming us to his company, and the tour. He introduced himself as "Eddie," like "Eddie Murphy" he said. I just chuckled since I thought he looked more like a teen-aged Jackie Chan. Eddie told us he could speak English, and that he would be our guide for the tour. He added that we were staying in the van for the whole trip; not the big bus that was promised to us in the brochure *(no surprise there)*.

I tried to nod off again, but the bouncing van and constant yapping from the foreign group behind me made it impossible. When ever the van would hit a bump it would keep bouncing for another 30 seconds. Eddie would hold up his left hand in the air until the bouncing stopped. He did this several times, twice before the bumps, as a warning perhaps? I just closed my eyes trying desperately to get some beauty sleep. The sun started to come up and the Golden Girls came to life. They were three elderly black women from the U.S, all widows I think. They all took their cameras out, and got into a photo contest to see who could capture the most pictures of the rising sun through the tinted windows as the van bounced along. If they hung out and drank all night at the bars in Pataya, seeing a sunrise wouldn't be such a big deal.

My own thoughts were distracted by the loud chatter in the back seat, and paparazzi like frenzy of the girls, but I heard the sound of a rooster crowing! How the hell could that be possible from the inside of a van going fifty mph? Ah, of course...it was Eddie's mobile phone's ring tone. Perfectly timed with the sunrise! I watched Eddie while he chatted on the phone, and I noticed he kept checking himself in the side view mirror. It seems that Eddie couldn't get his hair just right, bed head perhaps? After fussing with his hair, he pulled out a wet nap and washed his face, neck, and arms; I guess he didn't have time for a proper shower before

56

he left for work. The Golden Girls had caught on to Eddie's shenanigans by now and we all chuckled together. I made some sarcastic remark about his sponge bath; I could tell by their cackling that they appreciated my sense of humor and we would get along just fine.

As pangs of hunger started to overcome me I recalled the travel agent at my hotel had told me breakfast would be included with the tour. Of course the hotel's breakfast buffet was not open yet, when I left in the middle of the night. Eddie helped himself to some sort of prepared sandwich; I inquired about our included breakfast. Someone in the back barked out in my support. Eddie just looked back at us and said, "Ok, 5 minute for Pee Pee and Poo Poo," I shit you not! (*No pun intended*). He wheeled into the next available service station where we had to fend for ourselves; scrounging up some food. I should have known better when I asked if breakfast was included and the guy said yes; they always say yes when they don't have a clue what you're asking.

Getting back in the van after the potty break I bitched to Eddie about the problem with my seat. He flipped it back and forth several times and then professionally announced, "It's broken." No shit Sherlock! He managed to lock the seat back into a 45 degree angle and motioned for me to get back in. It seemed Eddie's English was pretty well limited to the introduction he had rehearsed; he just looked at us whenever we asked him anything. The pit stop was a perfect opportunity for Eddie to polish up the Dirty Harry pair of shades he was now sporting. The sun rising sun was behind us, but I guess it kept getting in his eyes when he fixed his hair in the mirror.

One of the Golden Girls screamed out in excitement at the gargantuan three headed elephant, mounted up on a pedestal, off the highway. This is a sacred beast to the Thais. Eddie wheeled us over to the shoulder of the six lane highway and told us all to get out for a "Peeture." All eight of us jockeyed for position on the narrow shoulder, as not to get run over by the huge trucks zooming by. I continued to fight with my seat and get laughed at by the other passengers. The next stop was at a wood carving place. There were a whole bunch of wood carvers working on some very beautiful wood carvings of all shapes and sizes. There were even life sized, carved elephants! The group was then separated; most went on to an Elephant sanctuary, and rafting trip.

I didn't think the hot and humid weather would be conducive to climbing on a smelly elephant in the jungle, so I opted for the Tiger temple (*the girls later confirmed I made the right choice*). It is actually an animal sanctuary run by Buddhist Monks; they've taken in sick, injured, or orphaned jungle animals. No one had bothered to tell me when I booked the trip that you shouldn't wear any bright colors; that the tigers might mistake you for a piece of meat. I was wearing a bright red "Tiger Beer" shirt that I thought would have been so appropriate.

There were lots of wild animals roaming the grounds of the sanctuary but many were trying to find the shade like I was. The Tiger area was worth the trip. There must have been a dozen Siberian Tigers spread out around inside an old rock quarry. They were on heavy chains; a trainer personally attending each one. We were told they were docile at the time because they had just consumed lunch, and probably wouldn't be interested in eating us; it was their nap time. We lined up, and were then taken around by a trainer, who would take you to the individual Tigers for photo ops. Another trainer followed with our personal cameras taking pictures for us; they got some great shots! You could actually pet them, but only on the head; I was tempted to rub one guy's belly as he rolled over and stretched out, but the trainer didn't think it was wise. Not like your house cat I guess.

This was a two day tour so Eddie gave us a choice of hotels; it was either the very rustic floating bamboo hotel on the smelly river, or the new hotel with air conditioning, a hot shower, and TV.

Gee, guess where I stayed? The next morning we went into the national park where there are a series of natural waterfalls. There is a six km trail you can hike up, along the seven different levels of rivers, and falls. It was a fairly vigorous trek that the Golden Girls were a little hesitant of; apparently one of them had a heart condition so it wasn't a good idea.

It was s tough climb up some of the rocky trails, but each level of waterfalls was unique and picturesque. The pools were crystal clear, and you were allowed to swim in any of them. Some people did so, but there were a couple pools that had "kissing fish" in them. Sounds harmless enough until you saw the fish chasing people around and nibbling on them; a little freaky to say the least. I made it all the way to the top level, where a jungle river spills into the first falls, and a beautiful pool. The water was aqua blue in color, because of the white mineral deposits covering the rock bottom. Shady trees and shrubs hung over the pool making it some kind of paradise for sure.

We got back on the road and drove across some salt flats where you could see large bags of sea salt on display, and for sale along side the road. The next stop was in Damnoen where the Shang floating market is. This area is a crossroads of canals where you are ferried in a dug out canoe, with a powerful motor and propeller sticking out the back. They take you along the canals to a floating market, where everything you can imagine is sold from boats. Fruits and vegetables, fish, stir fries being cooked right on the boats, and cold beer on ice! You would think that would be no big deal, but then try to imagine twice as many boats as there is room for in the canal, jockeying for position to sell their wares. It is a virtual log jamb of boats, but a kaleidoscope of colored boats, and women wearing different hats that look like lamp shades. I bought a huge bag of saffron for two bucks, a cold beer from another boat, and some fried banana from yet another. All the while we were moving, and being bumped into; I was getting my goods and handing money from boat to boat, like when you pass the hot dog down your row at the ball game. I could never justly describe this place; it's one that you have to see to believe. The amazing part about it is that this is how the locals do it there every day.

The next stop was the Bridge on the River Kwai. The movie of the same name was about how Japan's prisoners of war built the bridge. It's not the original bridge since that one was blown up at the end of the movie. It is still a major tourist attraction. There is only the part of a foundation on one side of the river, that's part of the original bridge. You can walk, or take the tourist train over the bridge. The train will take you to the mountain pass where there's a truss bridge, and the movie "The Casualties of War" was filmed. The war was actually in Viet Nam, but that's Hollywood!

There was one final stop before we headed back home; the war cemetery where the allied soldiers were buried. The white headstones all in neat rows, with neatly trimmed green grass in between, was a somber sight. The cemetery was the transfer site for our ride home; where the big bus was supposed to pick us up. Nope, just another passenger van and a four hour ride back.

"Thanx Eddie!"

King Cobra

Hanoi, Viet Nam

"If you reject the food, ignore the customs, fear the religion and avoid the people, you might better stay at home."
— *James Michener*

I had been forewarned by a friend of the long ride into the city, from the airport in Hanoi, when entering Viet Nam. I was told to look for a shuttle bus that was much cheaper than a taxi. Of course, it was late in the evening, and not only could I not find a shuttle bus, but I could not find any signs of any sort, that might direct me to any mode of transportation. I cringed as I was flagged down, and then accepted a taxi ride with a quoted fare of $20 U.S. "No problem," said the guy who whisked me off to his friend, waiting outside in the taxi. I hate arriving at any unknown destination at night, or making any rush decisions in such a situation, but it was late at night, and I wanted to get to the hotel.

The taxi made an unannounced stop, and the gopher returned with a six-pack of beer....it seems they wanted to be my buddies; I knew where this was going, my fare was going up already. We came to a highway toll booth, and the gopher put out his hand to me for the fare. I refused and he said they'd get it *(another fare increase)*. I explained to them the area of the city I wanted to be in but they just stopped in front of the first hotel we came upon. This is where both the men lost their previously slight command of the English language. My U.S. twenty wasn't gonna do it and he basically told me my wad of Vietnamese Dong was useless. *(I had exchanged $100 U.S. at the Airport for 1.7 million Dong)*. I didn't like the time of night, neighborhood, or these two clowns who still had my luggage in the trunk, so I started to get out of the taxi, telling them the hotel would take care of it. I saw the hotel

manager inside and waved him out, telling him the taxi was trying
to rip me off. I offered up another $10 U.S. to get my bag in hand,
and I walked away leaving them to argue with the hotel manager.

The hotel was clean with hot showers, good Aircon; breakfasts
included, and free Internet; a deal I thought, for the same price as
the taxi ride! I started out with a fresh attitude in the morning, after
a lovely fresh fruit and omelet breakfast. I had found out earlier
that my first pension check had not yet hit my bank account. Thank
God for my line of credit! Hitting the sidewalk I was immediately
blown away by the traffic noise, and congestion that primarily
consisted of motor scooters. There was barely enough room to
walk; the sidewalks were parking lots for the scooters. I wanted to
stay in the area near Hoan Kem Lake, in the older, center of town.
It was hard to tell by the map just how far I was from the lake so I
accepted a ride from a cyclo-taxi with the quoted price of $15,000
Dong....somewhere around a buck and a half if I was doing my
Gozinto's right. My 10 minute ride ended with the guy asking for
$50,000 Dong, he insisted it was my misunderstanding of course.
A local walking by us overheard the conversation and shook his
head in agreement that I was getting fleeced. Welcome to Hanoi!

I was delighted to see the scenic and historic lake in the city
center, although the overcast and slightly foggy conditions stole
from its beauty. There was a wide path that went all the way
around the lake and looked great for strolling. I could enjoy the
peacefulness of the lake on one side of me, and the hustle and
bustle of the city on the other. I hadn't gotten 100 yards when a
local guy on a park bench made a comment about my camera. He
said he had some questions for me, and wanted the chance to
practice his English. Uh-huh, I'd heard this line before in Mexico;
they always work some angle to try and sell you something. I
humored the guy as I continued my stroll, snapping a few photos
along the way. He offered some free narration and facts about the
lake and its legends.

My new friend's narration soon turned into a spiel about the sites that "I should" see *(same ones recommended by the hotel)*. I asked how much that would cost and he said it was up to me *(yeah, ok)*. Of course, my new friend had his scooter waiting nearby. Sometimes you have to trust or rely on the locals to get the inside scoop, so I jumped on the back of the scooter, and away we went. The guy spoke pretty good English and seemed to know his way around. He started zooming down back streets and alleys to avoid the stagnant traffic. I didn't mind at all; it gave me a chance to get off the beaten path, thus quenching my nagging thirst for a new adventure.

We tore up some back streets and alleys, and ran over a few toes, you just honk and go; it seemed. All of a sudden we were at another small lake in the middle of an upscale neighborhood, with multi-level condos or apartments. It was Huu Tiep Lake, where the North Vietnamese shot down an American B52 Bomber; it crashed down right in the middle of this neighborhood lake *(no larger than a football field)*. The locals were so proud they have left a hunk of the plane there to this day, with a plaque commemorating the day they shot it down. Part of the planes fuselage and wheel assembly eerily sticks out of the still water, mirroring the surrounding buildings. There is a monument nearby on yet another lake where U.S. Pilot, Senator McCain was shot down, captured, and then held in the infamous "Hanoi Hilton" as a P.O.W. I wanted to see the former prison but it didn't fit into our agenda.

The Hanoi Hilton was closed for lunch; my guide asked me if I wanted to check out a local snake farm in the area, in the mean time. He assured me I could get a cold beer and a snack there so I agreed. The place looked like any other multi-level apartment building, but each floor had something to do with the raising of King Cobra snakes. The main floor had a display of several different pickled snakes, or snake wine in some cases. I thought I'd wait for a beer! On the next floor up a young girl appeared with a burlap bag, pulled a Cobra snake from it, and put it on the floor a bit too close to my feet. She taunted the snake so it reared up into the classic Cobra stance that we're all familiar with. The girl's mom asked if I wanted to try eating some but I said no, at first.

My guide said they cook the snake different ways and the woman told him she'd let us try "a couple" appetizers. I figured what the hell, I had eaten Tarantulas 2 weeks prior in Cambodia so what's the harm with snake? Agreeing to the snack meant we were shuffled to an outdoor balcony patio, where I was finally offered a beer. I had to request a glass of ice since I can't stand piss warm beer. I was just cooling off my parched throat with the beer when the old woman reappeared, snake in hand; she cut its throat right there at the table! She funneled the blood into a bottle and offered me a drink; no thanks, my beer was fine. Sensing I might be a true carnivore she then sliced open the snake, popped out its live beating heart, and put it on a plate in front of me.

O.k., I had to draw a line somewhere; I said I'd only eat the heart when it was dead and cooked. My guide challenged me, so I agreed to mix the snake blood with the rice wine, and I drank a toast to the King! The guide told me there were at least 10 different ways they could slice and dice that one snake into meals. This was all pretty interesting, and obviously future story material! While I tried not to swallow the ice cubes in my beer, the woman brought out two different snake dishes. One was fried with onions, and the other was barbequed....yup, kinda tasted like chicken! It was actually pretty good but it didn't end there; the old gal kept bringing out more and more dishes!

I couldn't help but wonder what all this was going to cost; it was way more than I had expected or asked for. I said something to guide guy but he was too busy stuffing his face and enjoying a beer on me. He only shrugged his shoulders when I asked who was going to pay for all the food that now covered the entire table....way more than "the sample" I agreed to. (*This is where you have to start wondering if this whole thing was just a scam to empty another tourist's wallet)* Sure enough, the bill arrived and my yellow guide turned whiter than me.... $3 million Dong!!! According to my calculations, this was just over $200 US dollars, a bit steep for lunch! If looks could kill, my guide just took a bazooka hit from me.

I counted on the guide as my translator, and I told him there was no way in hell that I would, or even could, pay that kind of bill; it was not even close to what I had asked for. He seemed quite embarrassed, and he emptied his pockets to the tune of 60,000 Dong. He also argued with the proprietor to get us another 30 thousand Dong discount because we didn't drink the various concoctions or half the food; the spread could have fed 6 to 8 people! The arguing continued over the huge shortfall; in fearing we might not make it out of the snake pit alive, I dumped another couple of hundred thousand Dong on the table, telling them that was all I had *(my U.S. cash was hidden)*. Soooo, if you've been doing the math, we were still well over 2 million Dong short!

I looked to my guide for some kind of escape from this huge mess; then he threw the keys to his scooter on the table. The woman wrote him some kind of receipt and we left on foot; the guide had PAWNED his scooter for our lunch!!! If this wasn't all real, it was some of the best acting I've ever seen; but hey, I've been punked before. I think I might have paid around $60 or $70 bucks in total, more than enough for a snake lunch I figured. We had to flag down a cab so I could get back to my hotel; my guide had the balls to ask for a ride to his apartment! I told him it had better be on my way, but he whined about being broke now, and how he would have to borrow money to get his bike back. Tough shit Sherlock; I showed no mercy and dropped him off with the parting remark that he had completely ruined my day! I was really pissed at first, but eventually shrugged it off as just another travel lesson, and another adventure tale for sure.

"A sucker is born every minute…was I one?"

Floating Junk

Ha Long Bay, Gulf of Tonkin, Viet Nam

"Like all great travelers, I have seen more than I remember, and remember more than I have seen."
– Benjamin Disraeli

Hanoi, Viet Nam was not kind to me during my stay, but it served me well as a base to use while I visited other places in the area that I wanted to see. I was told there are 50 million scooters in the country of Viet Nam, and 6 million people in Hanoi. I had to believe the majority of the scooters were in Hanoi. In considering the accompanying crowds and vehicular noise, I decided to get out of town. There are always plenty of options when you travel on your own with no set agenda, so I decided on a no brainer mini trip, where the itinerary is planned for you. I booked a four day tour that combined two days on a boat in Ha Long Bay, and two days trekking in the mountains of Sa Pa, in the north, near the Chinese border.

After booking the trip and spending the day wandering around Hanoi, I chose a restaurant just across the street from my hotel for dinner. One never knows when it comes to choosing a place to eat, but this one was full of locals; I took that as a good sign. I was still on my first beer when a black guy came in, I recognized him from my hotel. I offered him a seat at my table; he introduced himself as "Finnegan" from the United Kingdom. He told me he was originally from St. Lucia in the Caribbean, then here-located to London, England where he ran a "greasy spoon" type of restaurant. He spoke about how he just sold the restaurant, and of "a few" different women in his life; I wasn't sure if he was celebrating retirement, or running from women trouble. Either way, he was cool, and we both chuckled at how the restaurant staff was staring at him. Turns out black men with fuzzy hair are a rarity in Viet Nam. They called him "chocolate man," and the young girls wanted to feel his hair. Finnegan just rolled with it. I had to ask him what the hell kind of name Finnegan was, for a black guy from St. Lucia!

Finnegan and I bumped into each other again the next morning as we waited in the hotel lobby for our shuttle bus; we had booked the exact same trip. We spent some time on a bus that took us to the coast, and Ha Long bay. Stepping off the bus and looking into the bay was like looking back into history a hundred years. The bay was littered with Chinese "Junks" (*wooden ships*), and the wharf area was crammed, with more of the same. There were hundreds of the turn-of-the-century looking ships, some with their sails up, and on display. For those who haven't seen one of these ships, they are built of solid wood, with a shiny varnish finish, usually two or three decks high; some have giant pleated sails that look something like seashells. This was quite a contrast from the gritty and busy city of Hanoi!

Our tour guide waved us down on to the pier, where a dilapidated wooden motor boat was jockeying for position with about twenty other similar boats. There was obviously no method to this madness; all the different tour companies were trying to get their busloads of tourists on to the boats at the same time. The problem was that there was only room for two or three of these skiffs to dock and pick up passengers, but the little people are creative and impatient. The large waves bounced our boat up against the cement dock several times as the guides whisked us to the waters edge, and had us hopping aboard in rhythm with the waves, as not to fall in the water, or boat head first. Everyone seemed to get aboard in one piece; we headed out into the bay where dozens of Junks were anchored. We steered towards one of the larger and prettier vessels, but just as we got excited our pilot turned, and brought us up along side something a lot less dramatic.

Our boat wasn't as fancy as the one nearby, or the one in the brochure we were promised, but it was still very nice. The entire thing was made of wood; covered with a glossy marine varnish. We were seated for orientation in a large dining room with beautiful wooden tables and chairs. Our guide handed out the room keys to everyone except for Finnegan, and me. He had only one key left in his hand, and he told us to follow him to "our room." It was a beautiful room with two beds, but Finnegan and I just looked at each other and laughed uncomfortably. I told the guide that I liked Finnegan, but we had paid for our own rooms, and we'd rather keep it that way. The guide grumbled and groaned, then left us there while he disappeared with his cell phone to call someone in charge. He eventually returned and gave us each our own room. It seems they did have one extra room reserved for the staff, but not anymore! We figured that out later when we saw the staff sleeping on benches and chairs in the dining room, and other places on the boat.

We cruised out into Ha Long bay; the weather was overcast, with a light drizzling rain, on and off. This was very unfortunate since the scenic bay had looked awesome in the pictures I had seen in the brochures and on the internet during my research. Still, it was a different world; huge green stumps for mountains stuck up out of the water, and were scattered throughout the bay. There are some 1600 of these mountain islands, most of them uninhabited because of the rocky and steep terrain. We motored on, passing the odd fishing boat, little rickety wooden things with partial tin roofs for shade, and hand held nets. The fisherman looked like typical Vietnamese with black clothes and pointy, straw, lamp shade hats.

We dropped anchor out in the middle of the bay for the first night. Delicious meals were included and served in the dining room; some kind of fish with rice for dinner, and plenty to eat. None of the booze was included, but of course it was for sale. Finnegan and I each took a bottle of wine up onto the roof top deck after dinner to do some socializing and star gazing. We met a group from Quebec, and a couple from Ireland. When we weren't chatting we were gazing up into the sky trying to distinguish satellites from shooting stars.

There were two brothers from Quebec who were seeing their own things in the sky with the shit they were smoking; some kind of wacky tobacky (*not marijuana*) that they swore was getting them high. I was on of the last ones to remain on the roof; just before I left I remember being overwhelmed by the huge sky, and deafening sound of silence! The only thing I could hear was the water, gently lapping up against the side of our boat. It was a perfect setting for a great night's sleep!

The next morning, just before we pulled anchor, a woman rowing a floating 7-11 store pulled up along our starboard side. There are no stores or supplies within miles; this entrepreneurial gal would row around in the bay from boat to boat, selling everything from bottled water to batteries. The tour then took us in to a large island where we did some spelunking (*cave exploring*). When we got in to shore we were met by more floating mini markets, these selling fresh Oysters. Once again our skiff had to jockey for position with all the other boats trying to get us on to dry ground. A cave is a cave as far as I'm concerned, but this one was pretty huge and offered some great views of the bay, and the hoards of anchored Junks. Many beautiful shots of the bay you see in brochures are taken from this vantage point.

The afternoon was left to our leisure; kayaks were available, or you could go snorkeling if you wished. I chose to catch up on my travel notes on the top deck with the pregnant woman from Ireland. We caught some rays; the sun lit up the bay, showing off its natural beauty. The cruise back was uneventful, except for my amazement in watching our boat captain steer the boat from his bench/bunk with his feet, while he lay back sucking on his cigarette. Our group was split up and sent to our individual buses upon returning to land, depending on our next destination. The Irish couple was also going to Sa Pa, my next destination. We said good bye to the rest of the gang, and headed for the mountains.

"This was not the last I'd see of Finnegan."

Lands of Lam

Sa Pa, Viet Nam

*"All journeys have secret destinations of which
the traveler is unaware."*

— Martin Buber

The second part of my pre-packaged tour from Hanoi took me to the town of Sa Pa, at the foot of the highest mountains in Viet Nam, along the southern border of China. From Hanoi, I had to take an overnight train that leaves at 10pm and arrives at the end of the line in Sa Pa at 6am; piece of cake I thought. The train station itself can be unnerving; it is packed with people like tuna in the can, and there is very little signage for track numbers or departure times. I used the name Sa Pa and pointed a lot; I was steered to the right track and train, but we had to wait there to find out exactly which car to board. A conductor came along carefully examining my ticket; then he shuffled me to my car and pointed out my sleeping berth. This was a welcome site; I had a bad case of food poisoning and just wanted to sleep.

A noisy group of locals gathered outside my door, but it seemed I had the cabin all to myself. The train departed, and it wasn't long before I started to doze off. Just as I was fading into la-la land, some of the noisy group came into my cabin pointing at me and bickering amongst them selves. Sure enough, someone fetched the conductor, and he came in babbling something in Vietnamese giving me the idea I was not only in the wrong berth, but the wrong car! I tried to tell him that is where I was placed, but we could not understand a word each other was saying; I just packed up and followed him to another car and berth.

Oddly enough I ended up in a cabin with the couple I had a drink with prior to boarding the train. He was a seasoned traveler from Australia; she was new to the travel game, and from the Netherlands. I had sat with these two for less than and hour at the café, quickly realizing they were not getting along too well. It seems she thought the whole trip was going to be one big shopping adventure; he was trying to teach her how to rough it, while sight seeing and travelling by back pack. And so, the saga continued, while I tried to get comfy in my new bed, and sleep off my illness. It was obvious that the woman was half in the bag, but that turned out to be a blessing; she soon fell asleep.

It was some time in the middle of the night; I was awoken by the dingbat woman struggling with the lock on our cabin door. We had locked it prior to crashing and now she was trying to get out of the cabin. She grumbled and groaned, fumbling with the lock, and then she started kicking the door. For some unknown reason she picked on me, and started slapping my legs, telling me to wake up. I was about to kick her in the head when her partner woke up and unlocked the door for her.

I woke up when the train came to a halt in Sa Pa, the actual end of that train line. I went looking for my taxi that was included in the package, and supposed to take me to my hotel, but of course it was no where to be found. Some guy with a cell phone said he'd take care of me and call my hotel (*in very broken English*); then he crammed me into his 9 seat van with 11 other people, and asked me for money. I tried to explain to him it was included, but he didn't get it; I got angry and climbed out of the van. I grabbed another taxi, and then had the hotel take care of it when I got there. The hotel looked very nice; it was perched up on a mountain side, overlooking a deep valley, and huge mountains, off in the distance.

My tour included some mountain trekking; the "first part" was scheduled for that afternoon. As luck would have it, Ding and Dong from the train were on the same tour as I was, and they were still arguing! Our guide introduced herself as "Lam." She was a short stocky woman wearing her traditional village attire. She was from one of the isolated villages in the mountains outside of Sa Pa; each place has their own specific colored costume that the women make by hand themselves. The outfits are multi-colored, consisting of a blouse with vest, skirt and knee socks. Some of them have their hair done up in colored ribbons or hats to match the outfit. Lam told me it is the woman's duty to make her own outfit when they turn 12 years of age; they weave, dye, and sew together the whole outfit!

Lam took us on stroll part way through town, and then off on some side roads and paths that all seemed to go uphill. The trek afforded a great view of the valley, where the pink blossoms of cherry trees were in contrast with the green rice terraces. Water buffalo and oxen grazed along the slopes, and in one place a group of local men were busy chiseling out new terraces on the mountainside, using only hand tools! We walked through one of the more touristy villages; the women and children sat in front of their straw huts selling hand-made items from dyed and woven material and clothes, to wood and stone carved souvenirs. We took a beer break near a pretty mountain cascade and gushing stream.

Back on the trail Lam and I noticed the dingbat (*can't remember her name and don't care to*) kept stumbling and falling behind. It turns out that she somehow found another booze stop and she was corked. Lam had to make arrangements for her to take a scooter taxi the remainder of the trek, for fear she would fall or injure herself on the steep and rocky trail. I thought it was quite a good hike for one afternoon but Lam told me it was just a warm up, and she would see me first thing in the morning for "part two."

The evening was spent at leisure, and I strolled around town taking note of the small groups of colorfully attired women from the various different villages. Some were carrying straw baskets, heading home with necessities they had bought, and some were selling their wares along the sidewalks. I found a great perch on a patio to people watch, wet my whistle, and chow down for dinner.

Sa Pa is a winner hands down, for having the most colorfully dressed people I have ever seen!

The morning skies were thick with fog, I figured my full day trek would probably be cancelled. My guide "Lam" met me at the front doors of my hotel at 9am sharp and said, "We go now?" Thank God the dingbat didn't show up for this trek. I questioned Lam about trekking in the lousy weather but she just shrugged and said, "Maybe clear up later." I found Lam's command of the English language quite remarkable; she had learned it from chatting with tourists! She told me she had been guiding for two years to help the family; her husband tends to their home and the fields. She treks the mountains every day for $70 bucks a month! She said it was better than chasing tourists all day trying to sell shit.

Lam walked off into the thick mist, like a good trooper I followed behind. The fog was patchy and I couldn't see much; the hills and wooden shacks took on an eerie appearance. It seemed quieter than normal with the faint sounds of chickens or roosters muffled by the soupy fog. Anyone who knows me is well aware I'm not a morning person; Lam was not a chatter box, so we got along just fine. We asked each other the odd question as we strolled down the main road towards the hill villages. Lam's village was out there some where; her sister was minding her children while she was out working.

We were on pavement for about 3 K's then we stopped at a road side shack so Lam could get some sticky rice; I grabbed a bottle of water. I got swarmed by at least a dozen little nippers (*no pun intended*) who wanted to sell me a bamboo walking stick. One by one, they all approached me giving their sales pitch, like their stick was something different or better than the others. I was relaxing with my water when the oldest girl (*about 10 years old*) in the group took a tone with me saying, "You buy!" I said, "Why I buy?" She responded, "Why not you buy?" with some added snotty remarks in her own language. They seem to have the impression that all tourists are rich, and we should buy whatever they are offering, whether we need it or not. Lam understood I was not into souvenir shopping; she helped fend most of the peddlers off, she probably just told them I was a cheap bastard!

Lam said, "We go now," and the water break was over. We headed away from the road down some sort of goat path. The slope was a 45 degree angle, rocky, and slippery from the heavy fog. Hmmm, maybe I should have gotten one of those walking sticks! Lam just trotted down the path, pausing on occasion to look back and see if I was still on my feet. She never missed a step. She verbally noted that I had big feet, and that was good cause I could see them sticking out past my belly. It seemed we added some humor to our relationship, whether I liked it or not.

The path got worse, and soon rocks were all I was stumbling over and walking on. The fog started to blow around a bit from the slight wind coming down the mountain; I started to see some of the steep slopes, and magnificent rice terraces that were constructed by the locals. They have conquered the mountain, turning the baron slopes into viable farmland, complete with irrigation ditches, running back and forth in between the rice paddies. These terraces are all built by hand since there is no machinery to be had. They use the power of the water buffalo for machinery. It was February and the rice would not be planted in that area until April so the buffalo and pigs are allowed to wonder and graze the terraces, like living weed eaters.

Lam stopped at the edge of a steep cliff where I could hear the sound of rushing water below. She laughed out loud at some mountain goats scrambling down the nearly vertical slope. I couldn't see the bottom of the gorge for the thick fog, and I lost my balance for a second while trying to take a good look. Lam then laughed at me. I laughed back, and said she might have to carry me if I fell and got hurt. She responded that she would just strap me on to a water buffalo. We continued on with the occasional jab, now walking on the upper edges of the rice paddies; it was like walking on a mushy balance beam. I think Lam was just waiting for me to fall into one of the rice paddies. Good thing I left my passport and valuables at the hotel; I was just waiting to fall into the muck too!

We trekked through different villages where Lam pointed out the unique, colorful, and handmade outfits that were as different as rival hockey team jerseys. There are no roads, no hydro or gas, or luxuries of any sort in these villages. Everything that they have in the villages is carried there by the people, or their animals. I asked Lam why the little nippers running around never had any pants on, but she didn't answer; I believe answered my own question later when I saw a little girl squatting to pee near the road. Think about it; no bathrooms, no diapers or rubber pants, just squat and go where you want…no messy pants. With that picture in mind, our next stop was for lunch. To get to lunch I first had to cross a river by walking across a rickety, home made, bamboo bridge. Keep in mind that I am twice the size and weight of the little village people, and you'll understand why I was a little nervous making the crossing. It bent and swayed, and of course Lam just laughed at me from the other side of the river.

Lunch was surprisingly good; it helped that I was able to watch it being cooked. The produce was all freshly carted in by the locals. It was a bit cool, but the fog was moving out offering me a panoramic view of the mountain valley. I sat on a covered patio overlooking the river and a waterfall. From the river's edge the rice terraces climbed up the mountain thousands of feet, disappearing into the big sky. The soggy green paddies looked shiny; the powder blue sky above glowed like a giant halo over the mountain top. I shared some of my lunch with a cute little kitten that decided to befriend me, and curl up in my lap. I tried not to break the little plastic kiddy size chair I was sitting on; the whole patio had the same tiny patio furniture, about half the size of the cheap adult sized ones you can buy at Wal-Mart. It must have looked like my ass was stuck in a milk crate!

After lunch I mingled with the dozens of women from different villages; they were loaded up with huge baskets and getting ready to head down into Sa Pa. It appeared this lunch stop was some kind of trading post, or perhaps a rest stop along the mountain trail. I snapped photos of the vividly attired women; a couple of them sat along side the trail, hand weaving the same large straw baskets they used to carry their goods. Lam gave me the wave, and we moved on. We trekked some fairly level ground for a bit; it was a nice relief. We got to Lam's village that looked kind of like it had a road, but she said only motor bikes or good four-wheelers, could access the village. In the village, Lam handed me off to another guide, a little whipper-snapper of a gal; she was guiding a guy named Louie from Lichtenstein. Apparently Lam went to check in on her kids while she was in the neighborhood. She rejoined Louie and me a short time later saying that everything was fine at home.

As we neared the end of our trek Louie and I noted how we were covered in mud from head to toe, and our guides were perfectly clean. The four of us casually strolled to the next village where the tour ended. There was a giant swing that Louie and a little girl played on while we waited for our shuttle bus. I can easily say that without a doubt, the natural beauty and scenery I encountered, was unparalleled in any of my previous travels; I was completely intrigued and awed by the lands of Lam! I felt compelled to give her a great tip as we parted company in town, and I sought out a celebratory beer in honor of my 10k mountain trek.

"Travel and change of place impart new vigor to the mind."
– Seneca

Fresh Beer

Hoi An, Viet Nam

"Broad, wholesome, charitable views of men and things cannot be acquired by vegetating in one's little corner of the earth all one's life."
— *Mark Twain*

Hoi An is about half way between Hanoi and Ho Chi Minh (*Saigon*) City, along the west coast of the China Sea. For you couch potatoes who are geographically challenged, the area is also known as "China Beach," the name of an old T.V. show about the M.A.S.H. *(Mobile Army Surgical Hospital)* in Da Nang. It wasn't really on my list of places I had to see, but fellow travelers kept touting the place as the perfect spot to chill. Furthermore, "everyone" said it was the place to go if you wanted cheap, tailor made suits, or custom made clothing. The town itself is one of the oldest in country; I chose a hotel in the old section so that it would be easier to explore the city on foot.

Being a person who easily melts in the sub-tropical heat and humidity I chose a descent hotel with a courtyard swimming pool (*still at a fraction of the cost at home*). A cold beer, and dip in the pool were first on my list of things to do. As it turns out the dining room overlooks the pool so I was able to grab a sandwich with my beer; I called it lunch. It was mid-afternoon, and I had the pool all to myself. They told me the pool was heated; a common joke meaning it's heated by the sun. Except for the shrinkage factor, the cold pool and beer were a great welcome.

It was late afternoon when I ventured out of the hotel and into the street, armed with a map to navigate the labyrinth of narrow streets; so narrow you have to step back into a doorway to allow vehicles to pass by. As I crossed a busy street that was the unofficial gateway to the "Old Town," I was immediately blown away; the hustle and bustle faded to strolling pedestrians, on cobbled roads and sidewalks. Children played in the quiet streets, shop owners sat on chairs out front in the shade, and dogs lay sprawled out in the middle of the road. The buildings were all painted in pastel colors, like boxes of the assorted chalk you used as a kid to draw on the sidewalk.

The pastel walls were splashed with brightly colored Bougainvillea on the sunny sides, and a dark mould on the shady sides. It had a European flair with narrow streets, shuttered windows, wrought iron balconies, and river front boardwalk. There was an open air market on the river bank where wooden boats were all tied up; the local farmers sat cross-legged on small blankets, with their fresh produce on display in front of them. The women wore the typical lamp shade hats. Bicycles were the main mode of transport; the odd scooter I saw had to be pushed, in order to abide by some type of bylaw in the pedestrian area. There were restaurants opposite the river with great patios to people watch from, and to sample some of the local fare being offered. A sign that said "Fresh Beer" caught my eye, and a comfy patio chair caught my ass, while I sat back and decided I would be calling this place home for at least a few days.

I learned that "Fresh Beer" was their name for draught, or keg beer. I was pleasantly surprised to see the menus had some English conversions; I ordered a local specialty called "White Rose." This appetizer rivaled my buddy Ricky Lum's home made wonton soup! It was a home made rice noodle shaped like a rose blossom, stuffed with either pork or shrimp, and served with a garlicky black bean type sauce. They just melt in your mouth and were easily the tastiest dish I'd had so far in Southeast Asia. A tasty appie, a cold beer, and a seat with a great view of strange little people wearing lamp shades; what more could a guy ask for? I was one with the Gods of food, beer and wanderlust.

I was strolling down one of the narrow streets near my hotel later in the evening, ignoring the hostesses standing out front of their restaurants trying to lure me in, when the one said, "Hey, you come in, you friends are here." I thought that was a pretty ingenious line, but quite ridiculous since I had NO friends in Viet Nam. The woman was insistent so I smiled and gave her the courtesy of a moment of my time. She pointed to a table on the patio where a group of tourists were looking in my direction, laughing and waving. Sure enough, there was my old buddy Finnegan who I had met in Ha Long bay. He was sitting with two Aussie couples, so I joined them for some laughs, and some cocktails.

I hadn't really eaten dinner so I asked the waitress/owner if she had "White Rose." She said she did not, but she thought I might enjoy the stuffed squid. Boy was she right....it was delicious! The squid was stuffed with minced pork, carrots, celery, spices, and served with a tangy sauce. I asked her how she did the squid and she pointed to a sign on the wall advertising cooking lessons; she said if I wanted to know she would teach me how to make it. The place was called Café 43, it came highly recommended in the "Lonely Planet" guide book; the Bible for backpackers in S/E Asia. It was to become my new favorite restaurant and go figure, it was only stumbling distance from my hotel.

I had been hanging out a bit with Gemma, a young woman from New Zealand. We had met at my hotel over breakfast one morning, when I offered to share my table. Then I bumped into her at the beach (*ok, maybe I was stalking her*) and we got to chatting and hanging out. I blamed her for my sun burn since I spent more time exposed then I normally would; we chatted, and I baked in the sun! We had similar plans for touring the area, so we booked a tour to My Son (*pronounced Meeson*) together. This was a Hindu ruin site, similar to what I had seen in Angkor Wat, but about 400 years older. When we caught the bus in the morning Gemma was not herself, she had gotten a touch of food poisoning. I already had that displeasure previously on my trip so I gave her some pills, peace, and quiet.

The ruins were in the jungle and it was fricken hot; 34 Celsius according to the guide! My skin actually felt like it was burning when I stood in the direct sun! I was soaked in sweat from head to toe, and had to take pictures from the cover of shade. The ruins were not as impressive as the others I'd seen, partly because of their age, and partly because of the aerial bombing by the U.S. during the war. The government asked Nixon to stop bombing the shit out of the ruins so he complied, and sent another 10,000 troops into the area instead. The tour included a boat ride on the way back; it was a great way to cool off and take in some different scenery.

I decided to take up the offer of learning how to cook my own squid appetizer at Café 43. I met the owner/cook in the afternoon and she took me into the kitchen. I tried not to look shocked when I saw the simple kitchen, and her in are feet. There was only a sink, prep table, and hot plate, along with the chair she placed me in. She then said, "I cook, you watch." I was simply amazed as I sat there with a cold beer in hand, watching her work, and wondering how the hell she managed to feed a restaurant full of people from this kitchen! I offered to help with the prep but she said I should just watch, drink my beer; and then eat the squid after. O.K. I said, "Only if you insist."

The Café seemed to become a nightly meeting spot for some of the folks I'd met in town. Finnegan was ready to leave the next day; he was finally in possession of a few tailor made suits, and happy as a clam. I invited Tess, an English girl, over to our table and we got serious with a bottle of rum. We ran late into the evening; the owner's husband came out to the patio in his jammies but was too shy to ask us to leave, I offered to buy the bottle of rum from him. We took the rum up to a balcony near my room and I waved up Darcy, a guy from Calgary, Alberta. We sent off Finnegan in style, cleaning out the mini fridge in my room. Finnegan had been travelling abroad for a whole year, and he was finally going home.

After Finnegan left town, Gemma met some younger guys from her own country and disappeared with them. I decided to rent a scooter and drive up the coast; it was a Yamaha, fully automatic, for the sum of 8 bucks for the day, including the helmet. No deposit, no insurance, and no I.D required! I took it for a test spin down the block; when I asked when I was required to return it she just said, "Tonight." I headed for the coast, and then up to China Beach and Marble Mountain. A couple young girls on a scooter pulled up along side of me trying to make conversation; uh-oh, now what? As usual there was an angle, and the one girl took me to her parents carving shop. The girl showed me China Beach and the abandoned cement bunkers the U.S. army left behind after the war. She let me park at her shop while I went and toured Marble Mountain, a place the Vietnamese took refuge in caves, hiding from the U.S soldiers and their constant bombing. Out of frustration in not being able to rout the little people out, the U.S. bombed the shit out of the mountain until they actually blew a hole in the top, exposing the caves inside.

The caves that had once housed a make shift army hospital, now held for temples for worship. A heavenly beam of sunlight shined down through the hole in the mountain top, lighting up the temple below. It was like God was shining his flashlight down, through the top of the mountain, showing his followers the way to the temple. The walk up the mountain was a bit grueling but the views and cool breeze at the top made it all worth while. I could see for miles in either direction, along the shores of the China Sea, and the city of Da Nang nearby. I'm not much of a souvenir shopper but the carving shop had incredibly beautiful works of art. The carvings were all solid marble mined from the mountain. I bought two hand carved candle holders to remind me of the ingenious little people.

"Quiet colorful streets, great food, making new friends...these are some of the rewards of travel."

The Beach and the Sunset Bar

Phuket, Thailand

"Travel is glamorous only in retrospect."
– Paul Theroux

The Beach

I have read somewhere, perhaps in the "Conde Nast" travel magazine that eight of the top ten beaches in the world can be found in Thailand; it's too bad I'm not really a beach person. I booked a day long tour that put me on a yacht, in the Adaman Sea in Thailand. I do consider myself fortunate at times since some people only dream about seeing or visiting places like this.

The boat tour from Phuket included everything a sun worshiping, beach seeking tourist could ask for. There was sight seeing, island hopping, swimming, snorkeling, kayaking, shopping, and a lunch too. The boat was nice with an enclosed cabin and upper sun deck. I wasn't impressed that the air conditioning inside didn't work; it was 35 degrees Celsius, and that's just plain f*#@"ing hot in English. I opted for the roof-top sun deck where the breeze cooled my sweat and I couldn't feel the heat from the sun as much.

Our destination was the Phi Phi islands where we could find our own piece of paradise. The first port of call was Phi Phi Don, the larger of the two inhabited islands. We dropped some people off there and headed to Maya Bay on Phi Phi Le. For you movie buffs, or Leonardo Dicaprio fans out there, this was the film set for the movie "The Beach." As we cruised into the bay the tour guide pointed ahead to the famous beach that was a pristine and natural paradise in the movie. What I saw was a jam-packed, wall to wall mess of tourists and boats so thick I could barely see the actual beach.

We dropped anchor out in Maya Bay away from most of the heavy tourist traffic. We were told we could kayak, snorkel, swim, or just relax there. I am prone to ear infections when I snorkel in salt water without ear plugs; of course I didn't have any with me. I decided instead to swim into the shore of another little island, where I saw a nice secluded beach. Once I was in the water I quickly realized I didn't need a mask or snorkel. It was the clearest water I've ever seen; colorful fish, a coral reef, and the sea bottom at thirty or forty feet below were all clearly visible. I have never experienced sea water that warm, it was barely refreshing.

The shoreline always seems closer than it really is and it was a tough swim but I managed to make it there without swallowing too much salt water, or getting eaten by any sharks (*we were told there weren't any around there, just like in the movie*). As I approached the beach I was gently washed ashore by the incoming waves. The whole bay was a perfect turquoise color. I planted my feet in the warm white sand that felt, and looked like baby powder. I swam to the beach; it is part of a small horse shoe shaped bay, surrounded by steep rock walls. A few others from the boat joined me on my piece of paradise, and some went to explore a cave just inland from the beach. Even though I'm not much of beach person, (*I hate the sand really*) the simple enjoyment of lying there watching my body sink into the sand as the gentle waves washed over me.

After my swim the boat sailed around the remainder of the island so we could see it in its entirety. I saw a huge cave that was visible from offshore that is used solely for harvesting birds nests for making "bird nest soup," a specialty in some Asian restaurants. The islands in this area are similar to the tall humps on a camel, and are sparsely scattered throughout the sea. We circled back to Phi Phi Don where a scrumptious buffet lunch was waiting for us. An icy cold beer and some chicken wings made me feel right at home. It was a nice break from the rice and veggies. There was more time to lic on the beach; this time I nestled myself in amongst some young, topless, female sunbathers who kept me distracted from the rest of the naturally beautiful scenery. It's a guy thing! If I went on about the contrast of the bright red hibiscus, planted in neat rows in the forest green grass, with the backdrop of the white sand and turquoise blue water, you would start to wonder about my manliness.

The island harbor is scenic in itself, with all the colorfully painted wooden boats, all in a perfect line along the beach. The wharf is a bit hectic with all the large boats lashed together for the lack of docking space. Imagine that feeling when you know you're drunk, and you have a bad speed wobble when you walk. This is what it's like walking over and across the several other boats you have been tied up to. You just have to try and remember which one is yours so you leave on the right boat. There was even time allowed for some shopping, if you so desired. Even though I'm not a shopper or souvenir hunter, I broke down and scored a pirated DVD of "The Beach" for three bucks. The late afternoon sun and breeze on the way back assured me I'd need a siesta upon returning home.

The Sunset Bar

Patong Beach, on the Island of Phuket is one of the areas that got nailed by the Tsunami in 2005. I was there only four years later and with the exception of a few photos around town, you'd never know what had happened there. There is a great boardwalk and main road that runs the entire length of the beach, but the night action is on Bangla Street. This street transforms itself from a busy commercial area during the day, into a gritty neighborhood with a carnival atmosphere at night. The street is blocked off by police at the beach road and it becomes a sea of nocturnal beings at the onset of darkness. The neon lights take over for the sun and lure you to dozens of restaurants and bars.

The bars are lined up side by side, each sporting their own names and signs, and they each have their own particular music blaring. They also have their own set of hostesses, or bar girls that try to lure you in to their particular watering hole. The bars are all about the same size, just small store fronts hollowed out, that maybe hold about forty people each. Some have bar stools or tables that spill out on to the sidewalk for a little extra seating or breathing room. I'm not sure if it was the music or a particularly cute hostess, which made me choose the "Sunset Bar" as my regular watering hole.

A hostess named Lucky became my new bff; *(best female friend)* she immediately impressed me by offering me a large refrigerated wet towelette, along with an icy cold beer. It was quite obvious that Lucky knew exactly how to win over a hot, sweaty, and thirsty guy. Seating me under a giant fan near the street where I could watch the action also helped. People watching seemed to be a national sport here, and Bangla Street was a perfect place for me to partake in the event. People from all over the world wander up and down the street here. There are more tourist gimmicks than you can imagine; one particular guy caught my attention, the lizard guy.

This local dude had a huge green Iguana that he would place on you shoulders for photo ops, and money of course. The hilarious part was watching him come up behind unsuspecting female tourists, and seeing them freak out when they felt, and saw what was on their shoulder.

Actually, I didn't see the big deal since I got to babysit "Barney" the Iguana when the owner wanted to drink, or have a bathroom break. Barney would just sit there quietly with me watching the girls go by. He was quite harmless really; too bad he didn't drink beer. Then there was the cigarette guy; he came by at least a dozen times a night to ask if I wanted to by smokes. I think I was there 5 nights and he still asked me every time he came by. I should have gotten Barney after him. I also met Maria from Finland at the bar, and we got to be nightly regulars. We would chat and compare each other's day, just like an old married couple. I didn't find out until after I returned to Canada and received an email from her, that she appreciated the fact I never hit on her; she was a Lesbian. She just enjoyed hangin, drinkin, and laughin with me.

"Bangla Street" and the "Sunset Bar" were rowdier on some nights, more than others. On one particular night I heard the bell ringing at the bar; if you want to buy the house a round you ring the bell. Strange I thought, but after enough "Smirnoff Ice" one night I found myself ringing the damn thing. It only cost me a fixed rate of a thousand baht or around thirty-five bucks for the round, some kind of watered down shooters. Munchies are also available as in any bar, and Lucky surprised me one night by offering me a handful of what I thought were very spicy peanuts. It turns out they were what we call "Carpenter ants." Not bad with beer actually.

I learned how differently things work in Thailand, especially when it comes to trying to hook up with one of the bar hostesses. They are there to seat you, get you drinks, chat you up in broken English, offer you half-ass back massages, and personally serve you in any way they can to make tips. Before you let your imagination run off, you should know that if you want one of these girls to leave with you there is a "bar fine" that must be paid to the owner or manager. If you pay the bar fine then the girl is free to leave with you and make any other arrangements that the two of you might agree on. So yup, prostitution is supported by the bar. There is no social security system in Thailand so many of the girls work this way to support their families.

After becoming a regular at the Sunset Bar and befriending Lucky, I learned that she had "a boyfriend" (*lol*) in Calgary who was sending her monthly checks to keep her from prostituting herself to other men *(dumbass!)*. Apparently this is quite common, and I heard that some gals have more than one sucker on the line. Men can be such saps. Yes, ok, I know you are reading between the lines here so yes, I did my part to help Lucky out with her family obligations. I offered only hard cash for mom and dad, and no personal bling for Lucky. I had wondered why one of the other gals made the comment, "oh-no, another Canadian."

I would be remiss if I did not mention the "Lady-Boys" of Thailand. I have seen Transvestites in other countries, but Thailand has the best looking men who've converted to women hands down! There was a cabaret style bar across the street from the Sunset Bar where the Lady-Boys were all decked out in evening gowns, dancing on the roof top. Maria coaxed me into taking some pictures with some of them. The one's voice was deeper than mine but he/she was hot! Some of these men have actually gone through, or partially gone through medical procedures to convert themselves into women. I saw some of them while I was completely sober, one night at a show; it was nearly impossible to tell the difference. I heard one scary story from a friend about a guy who fell in love with, and actually proposed to a gal, only to find out she was really a he! *(The movie "The Crying Game" was something along those lines)*

Nights could almost become days on Bangla Street; the bars never really close until everyone goes home. You would see the crowds thin out, and then eventually the die-hards would stagger home. This was life and a nightly routine for girls like Lucky, and her friends. It was the circle of life in Thailand where different tourists such as me come and go, and the circle goes on, and on. Such is real life in Phuket.

High Good-Bye

To say good-bye to Phuket and Thailand, I decided to rent a motorcycle on my last day to tour the island. My friend Lucky was supposed to act as my tour guide, but I gave up waiting for her and departed solo at noon. $600 baht or about $20 bucks got me a 400 or 450 cc Honda; it was hard to tell, it was about one third the size of my Harley at home. A passport for I.D. was all they looked at, no driver's license or insurance nonsense to worry about. The real challenge was going to be driving on the right side of the road in the city, and then switching to the left side outside of it, yeah-huh, it made perfect sense to me!

It's all uphill heading out of Patong Beach; the nicely paved roads wind their way along the coast, and up into the mountains. The scenery was beautiful; it rivaled the Mediterranean Sea and Pacific coast in the U.S. The bike itself, and steep roads were a challenge with a crappy carburetor, and lack of shocks; it was quite evident when I hit the odd surprise pot hole. I found the highest peak on the island where a scenic overlook allowed me to gaze over the miles of magnificent beaches and coastline. I covered the whole south end of the island, and then went north and found a nice shady lunch stop on a touristy beach. The restaurant was completely constructed under some type of gargantuan tree. The bar tender told me this beach area fared well during the tsunami because of the deeper water out in the bay.

> *"Life is a beach, I'm just playing in the sand"*
> *– Lil Wayne*

My Gym

Windsor, Ontario

*"People travel to faraway places to watch, in fascination, the kind
of people they ignore at home."*
— *Dagobert D. Runes*

This story is a little different in that it's not about one of my
trips or adventures but simply about a place close to home
that many of us health conscious freaks can relate to. The Gym is
certainly a place to go if you wish to torture your body, in the hope
that it will reward you with a longer and healthier life. It is a place
for some to socialize, and even show off the latest fashions in
sports attire. I go to the gym to keep from getting any fatter than I
already am, but I must admit to occasionally socializing there. And
of course, I find the gym another great place to people watch while
I'm grunting, groaning and sweating profusely.

In the old days gyms were strictly for the Arnold
Schwarzenegger types, a place for men only where you could dress
the way you wanted, sweat all over the equipment, grunt or yell
profanities, fart out loud, or even bang a few steroids with your
muscle head buddies. Like the rest of the world, gyms evolved into
a kinder and gentler place where women were admitted in, and
guys had to start wearing sleeves and wiping up their sweat. It was
a slow transition where the gyms offered women only rooms at
first, but eventually the women migrated to the men's room to
check out the buff guys. Men's workouts would never be quite the
same once the women in spandex started stretching and bending
over in front of them, a hardship us men have had to learn to cope
with.

I have worked out in many places ranging from my own home
to the mega-gym style places like the one I'm at now. These mega-

gyms offer every kind of exercise equipment you can imagine, along with swimming pools, saunas, tanning beds and even massage chairs. My gym even has a Chiropractic office in the building. For my personal amusement, my gym comes equipped with a wide variety of characters for me to watch, and wonder about while I am in the fat burning zone. I'll describe a few for you.

The Queen

I chose to start with "my friend" because she is the social glue that holds our gym together. I had met her when I was a teenager when, as she says, "her dad was banging my mom." It's just her way of telling people that our parents dated long ago, and how we could have been brother and sister. Turn's out I also know her husband and brothers. I love her perverted and twisted sense of humor; it is just like mine, perhaps we really are related. She knows everyone who works out before noon, and if you want the scuttlebutt on anyone, she is the one to ask. She somehow manages to actually get sweaty, and stay updated on the latest gossip, all in her short four hour routine. My bff *(best female friend)* is almost as old as me, yet she looks great in her spandex, and has a flock of drooling old men that follow her around the gym. She basks in the attention yet is a loyal loving wife whose only complaint is that she never gets enough from her man *(God bless her soul!)*.

Bucky Bug-eyed Guy

One of the first characters that caught my attention at this gym was a guy who gives me inspiration. He's got to be 60ish, with a great beer belly that he likes to accentuate by wearing a tight weight belt over his skintight, and tucked in shirt. He tried to make conversation with me once but I couldn't look straight at him without cracking a smile. His thick glasses and bulging blue eyes *(one blew east and one blew west)* look like those gag glasses where your eyeballs pop out on springs. He's got a gap in his front teeth you could spit a peach pit through, and his conversation always goes something like, "Hey, how bout that hockey game eh?" He has a wad of thick black hair hanging out of each ear that looks like fuzzy caterpillars trying to escape. He is bow legged and walks with his arms out like his chest is too wide for his body. Actually I think it's his belly that keeps growing, regardless of his working out.

Hanson Brothers

Well, almost the Hanson's; they just don't have the glasses, they probably wear contacts. I would never make fun of an invalid but I've noted these guys as a group; by their similar looks, they have to be brothers, and perhaps triplets. Actually, the brother in the wheel chair is the most handsome of the three. The next brother is always there with him and I swear he still uses a bowl for his haircuts, like "Moe" of the "Three Stooges." They always seem to be at the gym the same time as me, and jockeying for the same machines. Just when I figured the two had to be brothers' a third one came in, and they were three. All have very bad hair cuts, the same spare tire around the waist, double chins, beady eyes and overall demeanor. I hope they got a good family rate.

Old Karate Kid

I can't really say too much about this guy except he looks just like the "Karate Kid" would now, 30 years after the original movie. His tee shirt is always out of whack and looks like a karate Gi *(the thing with the belt)*. His hair is greasy straight and not too long, kinda like the kid and he always, always, wears a bandana.

He never, ever talks to anyone and walks something like "David Carradine" in "Kung Fu." He's looked in my direction a few times but I don't think he sees me; I think he's in some kind of trance.

Russian Princess

Thank God for women like the Russian Princess who keeps the men distracted and the women disgusted. She is thin, with platinum blonde hair *(sometimes with pink highlights)*. She has a different color spandex outfit with matching sneakers, head band, gloves, and sweat towel, for every day of the week that she is there. My fashion consultant at the gym tells me that money is no object when it comes to the Princess' wardrobe. She makes sure that her clingy stuff is quite revealing in all the right places and she seems to spend a lot of time on the machine where you sit and spread your legs as wide as they go. This machine is strategically positioned facing the isle for a better male perspective, of course. I've also have it from a good source that this woman is married, but quite happy to give certain men private, personal training outside the gym.

Coffee Guy

I finally got a chance to chat with this guy a bit one day when some poor old guy had a stroke and was carried out by EMS. The week before that a guy dropped dead from a heart attack; they say this working out shit is good for you! Anyway, Coffee Guy made some comment about how low the old guy's blood pressure was. I asked him if he was there every day since I always see him there, no matter what time I go. He said, "Yeah, do ya think I wanna end up like that guy?" Coffee Guy always seems to have one in his hand or near by. I've heard he actually is in there every day, all day, and that he has no life. Go figure.

Preacher

I haven't seen the Preacher in awhile....damn, no wonder my soul feels tarnished. This guy used to be in there the same time as me all the time but then I heard from a buddy he was in there at night. Guess those night owls need some soul cleansing too. This guy is at least 6'-4" tall and pretty fricken big, with an even bigger voice. He likes to shout out across the whole gym to someone if he is talking to them. The one time I worked out beside him I discovered his body odor was pretty big too. He even had a big hairdo but then took it down to the wood, must have been penance for something. I listened in once when he loudly preached to, and tried to hit on some poor woman who did her best to nod and try to ignore him at the same time. I'm not sure if it was his preaching or rude flirting that turned her off the most.

Sponge Bob

This guy is probably 60ish, in great shape, and is in the gym most days I'm there. He has the straightest long white hair I've ever seen, kind of like Hulk Hogan's in his later years. Sponge Bob seems normal enough to me except for the green and yellow sponges he carries in each hand. I can't help but wonder every time I see him why the different colors, left and right perhaps? He does have a practical use for the sponges; I've seen him using them as grips in his hands when he uses the machines or dumbbells. I guess they're softer and more absorbent than work-out gloves. One would think he would at least have a matching set! Perhaps he should talk to the Princess.

Mohawk Trainers

I was starting to think it was a prerequisite for being a personal trainer that you had to have a Mohawk haircut to go along with the abusive steroid look when I first joined my gym. Just when the one guy shaved his off another guy would pick up the torch. I just love watching these guys when they're working out on their own time. They scream loud enough to rattle the mirrors they're staring into, and when they drop the thousand pound weights it knocks stuff off the shelves in the Dollar Store below. I guess they are not as strong as they look since they can never pick up the weights when they're done with them. The new fat women members love signing up with these guys for personal training. If one of these guys ever smiled or said hello to me I'd go buy a lottery ticket.

Where are the Hotties?

I would have to think that the object of everyone who goes to the gym is to become somewhat healthier, and to feel better about themselves. I would also think that you would look to the employees and trainers at the gym to set an example and help you in accomplishing your goals in that regard. Why then, does my gym have "some" of the fattest, ugliest female employees anywhere? Not only are these women a little more than overweight with rumpled clothes, some look like they haven't washed their hair in days, or ever tried putting a simple splash of make-up on. In fairness, the personal trainers are pretty fit overall but it's the girls who work right up front and center when you walk in. Add them to the gay guy (*with a Mohawk*) who chain smokes out front when he's on his breaks and it gives me all the incentive I need! Looks can be deceiving though, he's the most cordial employee there!

Old People

I had to hurry up and write this before I become one of those old folks I see every day doing water aerobics in the swimming pool. I always pause and take a look at this crew exercising; I think it looks like a scene from that movie "Cocoon." Everyone is continuing in their pursuit of putting a few more notches on that tree of life. I do find it very revealing since it is a window to my own future where I can see what I'll look like in another 20 or 30 years, where exactly the rolls and wrinkles will be, or which body parts will no longer operate efficiently. It's a kind of a Catch 22 I guess, you don't know if it is depressing, or an incentive to do your best in not letting it happen to you. Such is life at the gym.

"Live long and prosper" - *Spock*

Rocky Mountain High

Rocky Mountains, Colorado

High Flight

Oh! I have slipped the surly bonds of earth
And danced the skies on laughter-silvered wings;
Sunward I've climbed, and joined the tumbling mirth
Of sun-split clouds – and done a hundred things
You have not dreamed of – wheeled and soared and swung
High in the sunlit silence. Hov'ring there
I've chased the shouting wind along, and flung
My eager craft through footless halls of air.
Up, up the long delirious, burning blue,
I've topped the windswept heights with easy grace
Where never lark, or even eagle flew –
And, while with silent lifting mind I've trod
The high untresspassed sanctity of space,
Put out my hand and touched the face of God.

John Gillespie Magee Jr.
RCAF Spitfire Pilot

I can only imagine the feelings that this man experienced and have often dreamt of accomplishing such feats but I'm not sure my earthly stomach could handle it. I have however, had my own defining moments while traversing certain places on my motorcycle. Although I think John Magee did an excellent job in describing his feelings to us, I know for a fact that unless you've actually flown an airplane, or have ridden on a motorcycle, you just can't truly appreciate the accompanying feelings.

Colorado Ted

A few years before this trip, I was in Cambodia and was introduced to Colorado Ted by my buddy Michael. Ted and Michael acted as my road crew in Cambodia when I rented a Harley and was escorted cross country by Alaska Mark. I later spent some additional time in Thailand with Ted who managed to show me some things that I had never seen before. Such is life in Thailand. Anyhoo, Ted extended an invitation to me to visit him some time where he lived in Denver, Colorado.

And so, the idea was hatched for a summer bike trip to Colorado. I don't normally like to ride the Interstate highways in the U.S. unless I have to be somewhere and need to make time. It was a three day ride to Colorado taking the old U.S. highways and back roads. Iowa and Nebraska were flat and mostly boring but that seems to be when my mind wanders the most, and I start to format some stories in my head. There may be nothing worth writing about at the time but you never know when a story will present itself.

Bridge Out

I had been following a storm for some time, somewhere in the middle of Nebraska so the roads were a still a bit wet in spots. I came upon some signs and a barricaded bridge that was impassible. The problem was I didn't recall seeing any previously posted detour signs and I had no choice but to turn around. I retreated all the way back to the previous town and took the first crossroad figuring I'd out flank the bridge by crossing the river further west. It was a lovely detour that did a huge loop through cow country and brought me right back to the same closed bridge!

Plan B was to head east along this road and follow the river until I came upon another crossing. The road eventually veered away from the river, but then I came across a good road heading in the right direction that "looked" big enough to have a bridge on it. It wasn't long before the road took a few turns into the middle of nowhere. Then I saw a sign that said "paved road ends ahead." No biggie I thought as I slowed to the appropriate speed and rode on the gravel. I thought I could see the river ahead and hoped for a bridge.

Just when I was getting comfortable with the gravel road it turned into dirt. Remember it had been raining and when dirt gets wet it becomes mud! Well, I've never ridden on a mud road before and it appeared that today was not going to be a good day for it. I immediately tried to gear down but dared not brake since I was already sliding in the mud and doing a low speed wobble. The front wheel was just plowing and the wobble got worse; I knew I was going down; it was just a matter of how hard and where.

I was sliding closer and closer to the big creek on the left since that's the way the road sloped. There was a grass shoulder where I thought I might get some traction or at least have a softer landing *(I really didn't want to crash in the creek)*. I slowly veered toward the grass shoulder and my front wheel started to grab the edge of the grass. The problem now was that my rear wheel was sliding up to the right. I figured this was the time to dump, so I let the front wheel grab the grass and I hit the rear brake as I let the bike flop down on its left side. The bike and I slid in the deep mud but I was able to use my left foot as a rudder until the bike came to a stop. I opened my eyes, took a deep breath and shouted "Yeah!" When I stood up I couldn't see my feet; I was ankle deep in the mud! The bike was sunk to the frame but all was good *(no damage)*. It was a perfect slide if there is such a thing. It was not nearly as much fun trying to get me and the bike out of the mud and back on to dry pavement. My wheels spewed up chunks of mud for the next 50 miles!

A Mile High

Riding into Denver, I didn't really notice the change in elevation; the road just gradually worked its way higher. I had heard athletes complain of Denver's altitude and how the thin air made it difficult for maximum performance. A useless fact that I didn't know was that one of the steps of the Colorado State Capitol Building is exactly 5,280 feet above sea level. That is precisely one mile for those of you who were brought up on the metric system.

I hooked up with Colorado Ted in one of his local watering holes.....exactly the same way I had originally met him. I was introduced to his buddies and I used a few cold ones to wash down the road dust. It seems Ted had fallen in lust since I had last seen him and he chose to spend more time with her than me; can't say as I blamed him. Ted introduced me to Ron, a fellow bike rider and we planned a ride into the mountains the next day while Ted was off doing his own kind of riding.

Ron showed me some of the night life in downtown Denver, and then we met at some greasy spoon in the morning for steak and eggs. We headed for the mountains through Boulder, then Estes Park working our way up into the Rocky Mountain National Park. I had previously travelled through the northern Rockies in British Columbia and Washington where the roads were limited and the terrain rugged. The Mountains in Colorado were greener with small villages or beautiful homes spattered throughout the slopes and valleys. The Alpine scenery is spectacular. The only drawback is that you have to keep your eyes on the winding road more than the abundant sights.

The loop Ron had planned took us up across some of the mountain tops that were over 10,000 feet high. The weather had changed *(as it often does in the mountains)* and gotten cooler. A light drizzle then made the roads a little slick but traffic was moving slowly and we managed to stay on the road. Another temperature drop near the top brought on a summer snow that made visibility a joke. The weather caused the fun meter to drop a bit since we couldn't see any of the scenery around us. We headed back down to Granby where the sun allowed us to dump our rain gear and we could once again enjoy the grand scenery. I think we were only about 10 minutes from Denver when the sky opened up on us without giving us a chance to take cover. Oh well, we just arrived home soggy! After the changes in the weather Ron added to my day of surprises by sharing his age with me. He was 72 years young! Cheers buddy!

Windswept Heights

With Ron's warm up mountain ride behind me I said my goodbyes and headed south to Colorado Springs. I had heard, and read about "Pikes Peak," its height, and the fact that you could actually ride all the way to the top. It sounded like a good idea and I do love a challenge. I found my way to Manitou Springs, a cool little town at the base of the mountain I wanted to conquer. It was a great walking town with shops and streams and boardwalks all entwined making for a pleasurable stroll for young and old alike. You can also catch the cog train from there that takes you up the mountain, in the case you don't want to drive a vehicle up. Apparently it is the world's highest cog railway.

I just knew I had to ride up that mountain instead of taking the train so I headed for the mountain and Pikes Peak in the morning, although I'd heard mixed reviews about the weather up top. On the road to the gate a cocky younger biker and his bitch passed by me on the curvy road like I was a slow moving farm wagon. He had the ape hanger bars that allowed him to display his arms; they were loaded with colorful tattoos. A short time later I caught up with him as we pulled up to the Ranger station at the gate. The Ranger explained how the road was only paved to about two-thirds of the way up the mountain but it was doable by car or motorcycle. She said that they had just sprayed the road with calcium to keep the dust down and it would be slippery if wet. The Ranger added that rain was expected in the afternoon…as always *(why didn't anyone tell me it always rains in the mountain peaks)*. The young biker dude chickened out and turned around.

I had read that the road up the mountain was only 17 miles, but the Ranger told me it would probably take an hour to drive it. I thought about that, along with the time spent on top, and then coming down, and factored in the afternoon rain shower. What the hell I thought, this was a once in a lifetime opportunity and I wasn't turning around. I paid my entrance fee and off I went.

The ride starts off at about 8,000 feet above sea level so it didn't seem to take long for the trees to thin out, giving way to thicker rock. The road weaved its way back and forth up the side of the mountain with 180 degree switchbacks and no guard rails. That really didn't bother me until I got up above the tree line and you could clearly see the sheer drop off the side of the road. I wondered to myself if anyone would ever notice me missing or even find me if I drove over the edge. The traffic was light on this particular morning but the odd gawker really made things difficult. I was riding in low gears, going up hill, in sharp banked turns; you can only ride a bike so slow before you lose your balance and fall over.

I felt the air cool and it got foggy but then I realized I was up so high I was just riding through the clouds! I had to stop and put my rain gear on but it never really rained as I continued up the mountain. I knew I was up very high when I started seeing snow banks on the side of the road *(in the middle of summer)*. The pavement was long gone but the hard packed road was still decent to drive on. Once I cleared the clouds, I could feel my ass cheeks tighten; it was a little un-nerving to say the least. The alpine views were spectacular; as my eyes were drawn out into the great expanse I started reciting bits of the poem High Flight that I recalled from Grade School. We had to memorize the poem for some reason and I had no idea why I suddenly recalled it. Perhaps it was just the surreal place I was in for that moment in time.

America the Beautiful

I came around one last bend and was on the top of Pike's Peak, 14,115 feet in the air. That's damn high in miles or meters! I parked the bike and walked around for a bit feeling a bit of heaviness on my chest. This was my first experience with the effects of high altitude. I saw the cog train that had to have come up on the opposite side of the mountain; I never ran across any tracks on my way up. Panoramic views in all directions were awesome and almost overwhelming. I could easily understand why this was the spot where "Kathy Lee Bates" got her inspiration for her song, "America the Beautiful."

People from all over the world go to the top of this mountain and that was evident by the assortment of State License plates. The ride up the mountain is not for the faint of heart though and I was a little shocked by one example of this. I overheard a group of bikers talking about the ride up, and how a couple of them refused to ride back down. They were going to take the train down and have their buddies come back up for their bikes! And here I thought, "What goes up must come down."

The ride down was a bit dicey for sure, trying to use the engine as a brake more than the brakes themselves. There was even a lane to pull over in at the bottom so the Rangers could check your brakes to make sure they weren't overheated or seized up. It was one of my most challenging rides ever!

"Now I understand why John Denver sang about the Rocky Mountain High"

On-line Dating

Lima, Peru

"Adventure is a path. Real adventure – self-determined, self-motivated, often risky – forces you to have firsthand encounters with the world. The world the way it is, not the way you imagine it. Your body will collide with the earth and you will bear witness. In this way you will be compelled to grapple with the limitless kindness and bottomless cruelty of humankind – and perhaps realize that you yourself are capable of both. This will change you. Nothing will ever again be black-and-white."

– Mark Jenkins

"Plenty of Fish"

The first stop on my South American adventure was to be Lima, Peru. I knew it was a huge city that would be difficult to navigate, and the culture shock upon arrival would add to the challenge. Then I had to factor in my minimal understanding and command of the language of most South American countries, Spanish. Thinking like a seasoned traveler, but also like a single guy, I thought a local tour guide of the opposite sex would make it a lot easier to acclimatize to the southern hemisphere. For those singles out there, I'm sure you are aware of "On-Line Dating" and the numerous Internet sites where we can all find our true love. Well, I thought why not search Lima Peru for a single female with similar travel interests who might want to volunteer as my personal tour guide. I logged on to the "Plenty of Fish" site and found Maria.

I had to chuckle when I asked Maria where I could meet her and she said, "TGI Fridays" at the Larco Mar mall. I am not a mall person, but was a little amazed to hear that a familiar North

American restaurant franchise was in Peru. Maria was an attractive woman, well dressed and well spoken. She apologized for her poor English, but it was much better than my lousy Spanish. We sat overlooking the Pacific Ocean while we sipped on some cocktails and got to know each other. Maria was a widow who had relocated in the U.S. with her American husband. Upon his untimely death she returned home and landed a good job in advertising. We got on quite well.

The City and the Mall

My friend Michael from Cambodia said that he had a love/hate relationship with Lima. I have to agree. The sheer size of the city with its traffic congestion, noise, and pollution left a bad taste in my mouth but like any other metropolis it has all the conveniences, and then some. I soon learned that the taxi cab was my best friend since they were dirt cheap, and the easiest way to get around. They did have some other ridiculously cheap mini buses that travel the inner city but they were always jam-packed with confusing routes. I found it much easier to show a taxi driver my destination on a map, then being yelled at by some kind of busboy who jumped off the bus and hollered at you to get on while pulling away from the curb with you only half way on the bus.

Before meeting with Maria and upon arriving in Lima at the airport, I had to search for my taxi that had been pre-arranged by my hotel. This was not to be the case so I got my own hack and showed him the hotel location on a map. No problemo. I was staying in Lima "Centro," the oldest part, and heart of the city. Things always look scarier at night and central Lima was no exception. The roads were in rough shape, there was lots of litter and garbage lying around and even the locals had a sinister look to them. The streets narrowed and the pedestrian traffic got quite heavy, considering it was ten o'clock at night. We started to follow road closure and detour signs, and I knew I wasn't going to like the outcome when the taxi driver asked for another look at my map.

My driver pulled to the curb on a barricaded street overflowing with people. He pulled my bag from the trunk and I knew the gig was up. There were no hotels in sight, let alone the one I needed to find. The driver helpfully pointed to a large public square that all the people were flowing into and said my hotel was just on the other side of the square; un-huh. Well, I was a bit kinked up from thirteen hours in the air, so maybe I needed a little stroll to stretch my legs. I travel light so my shoulder bag and little back pack on wheels weren't a problem, except on the cobblestone. I followed the crowd into the square. There were at least ten thousand people celebrating something that I was obviously not aware of. I headed for a traffic cop to ask directions but I was drowned out by the thundering fireworks that were being set off in the square. This was my welcome to South America I guess, quite impressive but a bit inconvenient.

I fought my way though the crowd and wandered around some of the side streets for at least a half an hour, getting some weird looks from some of the locals. I seemed to be the only silly gringo wandering around all sweaty and dragging luggage. I finally stumbled upon a taxi driver standing beside his parked car, and I asked if he knew where my hotel was. He pointed out that I was standing in front of it, and the door was directly behind me. Dumb ass! *(Me)*. The front door was part of what looked like a garage door and there was a car parked in the lobby when I went in. The clerk was shyly welcoming, and once I introduced myself he asked why I didn't wait at the airport for my taxi. He then called the guy who was apparently still at the airport looking for me. Dumb ass! *(Him)*.

The hotel looked dark and gloomy, but kind of like an old museum. My room was non-descript, but it had a bed, ceiling fan, TV, and shower, all for about fifteen bucks. I made a quick trip across the street to fetch a couple cold king cans, and some "Lays" potato chips. When I left my room in the morning I saw that I really was in a museum. It was an eighteenth century mansion of some sort, converted to a hotel. There was a spiral, solid wood stairway leading to a roof top patio where breakfast was served. The patio was covered with lush plants and vines, and it had a fountain in the center with a colorful parrot perched on it. It overlooked a large cathedral that was across the street. Later in the day while I was sitting up there journaling, a huge turtle the size of a dinner platter strolled across my feet! Must have been the hotel pet?

There was a covered courtyard in the center of the hotel with balconies outside the rooms overlooking it. The walls were adorned with huge antique paintings with gilded gold frames. There were also large statues, and antique furniture scattered throughout the upper floors. The central location of the hotel made for a great base to explore the city core and Plaza Mayor, the huge square that was the center of the celebration. I think it was some kind of Independence celebration; it included bands, parades and a bunch of race cars that lined up there prior to a tri-country road rally. The 17th and 18th century Spanish architecture around the square was very impressive. The hand carved wooden balconies that protruded from the second stories drew my eyes up and made my jaw drop.

My new friend Maria thought that my hotel was not in a very nice neighborhood so she recommended one in Miraflores, a more upscale area of the city. The Larco Mar mall where I met her was still a fifteen minute cab ride from there. My taxi driver dumped me on the street in front of some big name hotels right on the Pacific Ocean. When I asked where the mall was he just pointed towards the ocean and a wide paved sidewalk that ran along it. Was it a pedestrian mall? I didn't get it. Upon closer inspection I saw staircase, and when I got to a railing overlooking the ocean I couldn't believe what I saw. This mall was dug, and built into the 200ft cliff overlooking the beach and ocean! It had several levels, with stores, restaurants, movie theatres, and bars. This was not like any mall I've ever seen!

I was early for my meet with Maria so I perched myself on a bar stool overlooking the ocean. There's nothing like a cold beer and a great view to change your perspective on any place, even Lima. As I sat there a shadow overhead caught my eye. There above me were two Para gliders riding the thermals along the ocean coastline. Down below I watched the waves roll in while the sun set. The neon lights of the mall took over as darkness fell and I strolled over to the restaurant to meet my online date.

Things always look different at night and Maria showed me a place where darkness, water fountains, and some creative lighting could tickle my imagination. As it turned out the "Magical Water Park" was only a couple blocks from my hotel. There are at least a dozen different fountains in the park, with thousands of people of all ages there to enjoy them. The first couple of fountains on the walking loop were nice, but nothing special to me having seen similar ones at home or the huge one at the "Bellagio" in Las Vegas. The next one caught my attention; it was a large circular pad with water spouts shooting up from the ground in various spots. You see these things in the water parks for kids to play in. In this one, fully clothed adults and children alike giggled and laughed as they tried to dodge the water jets. Most of the water spouts were in rows and predictable, but there were other ones that shot on angles at random, eliciting screams and shouts of fear and laughter at the same time.

The next fountain was really cool, except for the long line up, and security guard with the irritating whistle. There was a tunnel to walk through where the water spouts shot up and arched over top of everyone without getting you wet. If not for the light mist or odd water droplet you would think the water was in glass tubes. I had seen one of these on a smaller scale in a park in Vienna, Austria, designed by some King with a sense of humor. There were several other fountains in a variety of shapes, sizes, and with colorful arrays of lights.

The thick crowds led us to the main attraction. This was a long rectangular pond with dancing fountains in the center, similar to the one at the "Bellagio," in Vegas. The dancing fountains and lights are choreographed to music, making it quite animated. Then just when you think you've seen it all before they take it up a notch. They had holographic images along with laser lights in amongst the moving water. The music had different themes; the images took on a life of their own to go along with it. The first was a dancing ballerina, and then other figures came; all dancing to the music in the fine mist of the fountains. Call me a big kid, but I was impressed. It truly was marvelously magical!

Taxis

I would be remiss if I tried to describe my Lima experience without talking about the taxis, and taxi drivers. I know anyone who has travelled probably has a favorite taxi story, and I have witnessed many of them in other countries, but Lima gets the number one spot on my top ten list. Like any other large city, Lima has some large roads and expressways; for the most part traffic seems to flow most of the time. It is when they have their rush hours or you get on the inner city streets where there are no traffic controls that it is just plain chaos. Perhaps to their credit, the taxi drivers always seem to be in a hurry, even when you are not, so you know you can't blame them if you are late getting somewhere.

It is their antics that make the Lima taxis, and their drivers stand out. Horns! Everyone in Lima loves to blow their horns. From what I could gather you blow your horn when you enter an uncontrolled intersection, when passing, to warn pedestrians to get out of your way, or in some cases, it would seem just to let everyone, or anyone else know you are in command of a speeding vehicle. I had to think even the locals hate the taxis; one I was in was actually bombarded with a full water bottle from an apartment building just before I entered it. The plastic bottle just bounced off the hood of the car. I didn't dare look up for fear of getting hit on the head. The driver paid no attention and just drove on.

My best taxi ride in Lima was with Maria; we were in no hurry, going to dinner I think. Traffic was bumper to bumper, and our driver already looked like a crack addict seriously "Jonesing." This guy was hunched forward clutching the wheel with both hands, and continually nudging forward inch by inch in the stagnant traffic. A small opening appeared in front of us in the left lane; he gunned it, but was cut off by a white taxi van that was quicker to the draw. Our guy was not happy and he let the other driver know it quite verbally! This set the tone as the traffic became more stop and go and these two clowns jockeyed for position.

Not to be outdone by the van, our driver started to look around like a "Bobble Head." He laid on the horn, then cut the wheel to the right and mounted the curb! Maria looked horrified, as we now were driving half way up on the sidewalk. We didn't seem to gain much ground, and it wasn't long before the white van was along side us again. Now the other guy was really pissed and he threw some paper garbage in our driver's window. Our driver retaliated by tossing his water bottle at the other guy. Even though my companion was mortified, I couldn't help but to laugh out loud since I thought you couldn't buy entertainment any better than this!

One more notable Cabbie was outside one of the Lima Bus terminals. I had just returned from a day excursion to Nazca, and I was trying to flag down a taxi outside of the terminal on the street. While I waited a taxi pulled up in front of me to drop a fare off. The woman had a few bags in the back seat with her and she placed one out on the street as she got out of the cab. As she turned and reached back into the car, the driver started to drive off while dragging the woman with the car! The woman screamed loud enough that the driver stopped within about 3 car lengths. I couldn't understand the Spanish the woman was shouting at the driver, but it was quite obvious she was very pissed off. The driver then looked at me to see if I wanted a ride....NOT.....I just waved him on.

"Lima, yes I loved it...and I hated it!"

Goose Bumps

Machu Picchu, Peru

"Travel is more than the seeing of sights; it is a change that goes on, deep and permanent, in the ideas of living."
– Miriam Beard

Goose Bumps

Why is it that all tours and excursions have to start so early in the morning? I boarded the bus for Machu Picchu (*meaning* "Old *Mountain"*) at 7 a.m. sharp. The weather was quite foggy and I could barely see the mountains that surround the town. It's about a twenty minute ride from the town of Agua Calientes to the Old Mountain. The bus ride starts out on the edge of town along the swollen and rushing river; the muddy water looked just like chocolate milk to me.

The rocky road gets steep quickly, and narrows to the point where you can only see thick vegetation on either side. I found this a little strange since most of it was growing out of, or on the rocky terrain. There were various colors of Impatiens and Orchids growing wild along the roadside. I had read that there are twenty-something different types of orchids that are indigenous to the area. Some brightly colored orange flowers easily caught my eye, set against the dark green foliage and shrubbery; it reminded me of the sun setting over a dark ocean, and matching sky.

The bus seemed awfully close to the rugged rock wall, and my window got splashed by a wild mountain cascade. The road weaved up the mountain with switchbacks that allow you to see the same scenery twice. The fog started to thin a bit and it looked more like clouds as we climbed higher, and higher, in the Sacred Valley. Yes, we were now at the same altitude of the clouds and as some of the dark green mountain peaks became visible the people around me on the bus fell silent. Only the occasional whisper could be heard. I'm not the type of person who usually gets overly excited about anything in particular, but in that moment in anticipation of what lay ahead, I got goose bumps!

Flag Wavers

The bus dumped us at the gates to the park where we were allowed to congregate while awaiting our particular guides. I had time to kill so I found a perch and decided to partake in one of my favorite past times, people watching. I listened and looked and saw people of all sizes, shapes, and colors. Some folks were attired more colorfully than the wild flowers along the road. I heard a lot of Spanish, but also English, German, French, Dutch, and some dialect from East Asia. A dog lay curled up and sleeping on the pavement in the middle of the mob of people, oblivious to our existence.

I was told my guide would have an orange flag so I moved to join his group. Hmmm, seemed to me he had just been holding a yellow flag. The guide then told me I had to join the group where the guide was holding a green flag. Our group followed the guide through the ticket gate where you had to show your passport to gain entry. Once inside the gate the guide split us into English and Spanish speaking groups. I was then to follow the white flag. For Pete's sake, I felt like I was in a "NASCAR" race!

A Lost Empire

The guide told us we would have about a five to seven minute walk to the viewing platform that would allow us all a spectacular picture for our "Facebooks." What he didn't explain to us was that the walk was pretty well straight uphill with lots, and lots of slippery steps. I was still feeling the effects of altitude sickness, (*my third day at an elevation of about 20,000 feet above sea level*) and had some difficulty in not only the climb, but just breathing. It feels like you have a piano on your chest and you can never quite catch a complete breath. Exertion only makes it worse. I was huffing, and puffing, and sweating profusely but when I saw an eighty year old woman keeping pace ahead of me I knew I had to suck it up, and tough it out.

We followed the path and stairs to an open area, or viewing platform that overlooked the entire Inca village of Maccu Picchu. It was like opening that best selling novel you've been waiting for, and turning to the last page. The tour guide mentioned he had a special connection with the Sun God. He then proven this to us as the clouds drifted apart for our viewing pleasure. I immediately felt small and insignificant. Once again the group fell silent for a moment until someone broke the spell and said, WOW! The guide let us stand there as he spoke about the Inca people; we just soaked it all in…. the landscape, the history, the moment.

There was still some heavy cloud cover obscuring a lot of the mountain peaks, but the clouds moved slowly giving me the sensation I was watching a 3D movie. The terraces that the Inca carved into the mountains stand out around the village looking like a giant "Lego" creation. You stand there trying to imagine flowers and crops growing on the terraces in such a harsh and alpine environment. The grey and white granite stones of the ruined village, all fitted together so precisely are so impressive against the dark green backdrop of the mountains. I looked over and down into the one valley where a bright rainbow arched from the mountain side, down into the valley where it ended at the muddy river below. Simply put, it was magical! It is no wonder the Inca called this the "Sacred Valley."

After seeing Maccu Picchu up close and personal I was both physically and mentally exhausted. I must say it made me feel "at peace." It was a soulful experience to say the least. A fellow Canuck who was standing near me at the end of the tour said it best:

"You just have to see this place to believe it."

Contrasts

Valparaiso, Chile

"To my mind, the greatest reward and luxury of travel is to be able to experience everyday things as if for the first time, to be in a position in which almost nothing is so familiar it is taken for granted."

— Bill Bryson

The bus from Santiago to Valparaiso was pretty uneventful in comparison to some of my Asian bus adventures. I had planned to ride the "Train del Vino" while in Santiago but it only ran on Saturdays; it was Monday and I didn't want to stay in town that long. I am a true Wino and had originally planned on touring some Chilean wineries but as fate would have it I had to settle for doing my tasting in restaurants. To put it simply, I found the city was just too big, busy, noisy and just not where I wanted to be at that point in my South American adventure. Don't get me wrong, I was impressed with the colonial architecture and I know the city has many things to offer but I just wasn't in the big city mood and I needed something smaller and more laid back; Valparaiso seemed like just the place.

I sat beside a local guy who appeared to be around my age but we struggled to communicate in broken English and Spanish. Language was definitely a barrier but I gathered that he was retired from the Chilean navy, and proud of his prior service. He was married with children, and he lived in Valparaiso. He was curious as to my plans and exact destination but we couldn't place it on my map so he used his cell phone and called someone at home to Google the street I was looking for. I had previously selected a couple of hotels up in the hills above town that were in my guidebook; the navy guy seemed obliged to get me to them.

Silence eventually took the place of our trying conversation and we both nodded off for a bit.

Valparaiso has taken commercial advantage of its position on the Pacific Ocean by becoming a major shipping port. In it's heyday before the opening of the Panama Canal I guess it was an important stopover for ships on the way around the bottom of South America. Logistics changed the shipping business after the Canal opened but the city has persevered. The port itself is home to several ships of the Chilean navy. One of the attractions I was anxious to check out was the dozen old lifts or funiculars that carry you up the steep hills in the city. There were over a hundred of these at one time, but with the advent of the automobile there are only a few left that are actually in use. How time and progress changes everything.

I traded the bus for a taxi upon arrival in the city and headed into the hills above the busy sea port. I hadn't bothered to reserve a room and took a chance at having the taxi drop me out front of my first choice of hostels. It happened to be full but the helpful owner directed me to another place around the corner. It was a warm and sunny day and I had no reason to fret so I walked over to the place she suggested. The "Allegretto B & B" was a quaint looking place, an old Victorian style house converted into a B & B. I thought I was out of luck again when I knocked and nobody answered, but then a head popped out of an upstairs window and the man said he'd be right down.

The guy that came to the door introduced himself as Ed, the owner; he said he could give me a break on the room rate since I was solo. The room looked just fine and the price was right so I moved in. Ed showed me the rest of the common area that included a kitchen and living room with seating areas. The decoration was a mix of antique and eclectic but so was the owner, Ed. He was an ex-pat from England who had fallen in love with a Chilean woman, married her, and then relocated to Chile to be with her and start a family there. The financial strain of the divorce had him running a restaurant and B & B to support the kids and his new life. Two things that caught my attention were quite unique for any kind of hotel. There was a piano in the living area and a huge coffee table with an ongoing jigsaw puzzle for anyone who wanted to join in. Cool concept I thought. Ed was also helpful with a map and list he had personally compiled of things to see, and do in the area.

It was only early afternoon so I grabbed my camera and headed out on foot to check out the neighborhood and surrounding area. The huge amount of graffiti on almost every building immediately caught my attention but there was something different about it in this town. There was the usual random tagging and ugly graffiti but in contrast there was beautiful and colorful artwork blended in with it. I headed down the hill towards the harbor but I was hypnotically drawn down strange alleys and staircases by the kaleidoscope of colorful and imaginative graffiti. I saw 17th century architecture with contemporary artwork painted on the facades of the buildings. Was it contrast, or irony in graffiti?

Every building and block was a new canvas painted by neighborhood or local, and unknown, starving artists. There were painted cartoon characters and Jesus Christ himself. Another was a painting of "The King," saying "Elvis is not dead." I saw new doorways leading to crumbling old buildings. I saw shiny new cars parked in front of 150 year old buildings. There were stray dogs and cats lying in front of fancy doors to nightclubs. I saw beautiful colored arrays of flowers spewing over old stone walls but then clumps of dog shit in the middle of the sidewalk; there was no grass anywhere. Exploring each block of Valparaiso was like opening that box of chocolates Forrest Gump was talking about.

My wandering landed me at the foot of one of the working funiculars Valparaiso is famous for. These things date from the 1800's and were used to climb the city's steep hills before Henry Ford changed the world. They are odd looking for sure but simple enough in their concept. From what I could gather, they are basically box cars on rails with a motorized cable system that pulls them up, and eases them down the hills. I don't think any of the ones I saw were more than a couple hundred yards in length, but the grades were very steep. Walking into the ticket booth was like stepping back a hundred years in time. There is nothing automated there with human ticket takers and change makers. The turn of the century machinery is still visible and in this case, and still in working order. The interior was very plain, basically a wooden box car with a couple of windows and wooden benches. With the number of tourists who ride these things you would think they could raise the 50 cent cost and spruce them up a bit.

There were the usual tourist traps at the top of the run, but a particular hilltop patio caught my eye. It was a pretty toasty day so the vine and flower covered patio looked like the perfect beer stop. There was nobody else on the patio so I had my pick of seats and I perched myself near the railing with a great view overlooking the harbor below. The contrast of this city tickled my brain as I thought about the old funicular, and looked down over a newly mechanized shipping port. There were huge cranes moving around steel shipping containers, stacking them four high like a child's set of building blocks. From the height of my vantage point the trucks looked like little dinky toys and the navy destroyers and frigates looked like plastic toys in a bathtub.

I worked my way back down another hill purposely losing myself in the winding streets and alleys musing at the new graffiti on the hundred year old brick walls. It was all so cleverly artistic, whether done purposely or not. Beat up brass and wooden doors leading to a trendy new restaurant, fancy banks with marble facades and grizzly old bums sleeping on the front steps. Even the squeegee kids had an artistic flair for soliciting funds in stopped traffic. These ingenious entrepreneurs had a timely act that had one of them playing a trumpet, while the other juggled three balls in front of the stopped vehicles waiting for the light. The actual squeegee kids just sat on the grass in the shade, perhaps awaiting their turn.

I did a loop through the tents of the various hawkers and peddlers down at the pier, just in case something caught my eye; I'm not normally a souvenir shopper. I couldn't help but notice some of the local street urchins lurking under a huge shade tree. One gal had pink spiked hair and so many tattoos it looked like her skin was actually blue. A couple of the guys were eying me up, and I could almost feel their hands grabbing for my wallet. What's an inner city of any type without scary looking people? The peddlers were not as pushy as in Asia or Mexico where you are constantly pestered. I couldn't pass up the smell of freshly cooked chorros and grabbed a bag. "Chorros" are made from dough that has been pressed into a tubular shape, about the size of a hot dog. They are then deep fried, and lastly, rolled in sugar.

I spotted another beer stop across the street from the pier with some locals who were whooping it up a bit. It looked like a perfect people watching spot with a busy sidewalk. Unfortunately the street was also busy with lots of noisy and smelly diesel buses zooming by on a regular basis. The warm chorros and a cold beer freakishly tasted good together, just another contrast in Valparaiso perhaps. I can't remember if it was the second or third beer when I noticed the waitress was getting pretty friendly with me. She was a very pleasant gal with a great smile, but that one missing tooth and the belly bigger than mine told me it was time to move on.

The evening brought on a search for an upscale restaurant in my neighborhood. I had seen a place called "Pasta et Vino" in a couple of guide books. Apparently it was a "must do" place with a great wine list. It was only a couple blocks from my B & B but for some reason I was having difficulty finding it. I stood at the intersection where I thought it was supposed to be with my head on a swivel. Usually my nose for food steers me in the right direction but I did smell food. There was a billboard on the sidewalk just up the block from where I was standing. It was not the place I was looking for so I stuck my head in the door to be nosy. A young guy intercepted me and introduced himself as the owner/chef; he said he could offer me anything the other place could...of course he could! Well, I couldn't find the other place, and I was hungry. Some times you just have to take a chance so I followed the guy in.

The restaurant was up on the second floor and I was greeted by a lovely young woman who just happened to be the owner's girlfriend. There was nobody in the place but I was early; folks don't eat in South America until after dark, sometimes as late as 11pm. The room was lightly decorated and looked fresh and new. The gal said they had only been open about a month and they didn't really have a menu yet...hmm, weird I thought. They did have a decent Chilean wine list and the chef came back to see me. We talked about a customized meal made to order in consideration of my cravings and likings. We decided on a surf and turf meal in a special mushroom cream sauce.

I sipped on a Chilean cabernet and was promptly served my appetizer. It was a plate of home made crackers with some kind of mayonnaise based dip; it was really good! I chatted a bit with the hostess until my main course arrived. The chef came back to my table and invited me into the kitchen to check on my meal and to let me sample the mushroom sauce. I couldn't identify one of the spices in it, so he explained its Japanese origin to me and actually bagged a sample of the stuff for me to take home.

"Accidentally stumbling upon something unexpectedly, can change a preconceived perception, of what you had previously believed."

Doors

*"One's destination is never a place,
but a new way of seeing things."*

– Henry Miller

Open the door.

What exactly is a door?

Is it really a portal to another place or perhaps another time?

Doors take you from the dark and into the light, from the cold to the warm, from noise to quiet, and from danger to safety.

Why do some people like taking pictures of doors?

Doors do take us places. We use plane and car doors to take us to those places.

Who were "The Doors"? Was Jim Morrison looking for the door to get out?

Many of us have wondered, what is behind that door, I want to know more!

The first porn movie was called "Behind the Green Door"

On "The Price is Right" they want you to pick a door.

In "The Twilight Zone" some plots revolved around tortured souls wondering hallways searching for the right door.

Who is behind those doors? Are they rich or are they poor?

Doors can take you home, to work, to school, to church, or into the dog house.

We use doors to enter a place but also to keep others out.

Why does floor sound like and is spelled like door?

If we choose a book by its cover should we choose a door for its décor?

Why does a door open in, if we are going out?

Close the door.

And then, there are windows.......

Mendoza by a Landslide!

Valparaiso, Chile to Mendoza, Argentina

*Writing and travel broaden your ass if not your mind and
I like to write standing up.*
— *Ernest Hemingway*

If you take enough long distance bus rides in other countries you are guaranteed some mishap or adventure sooner or later. I've had my share of memorable bus rides in Mexico and Southeast Asia, and now I can add South America to my list. Why would someone want to pass up such opportunities by utilizing expensive air travel with no panoramic views, or no tales of adventure that might come your way? I think taking a bus in some countries is like buying that box of chocolates; you never know what you're going to get.

It was another early departure with a hangover, thanks to my B & B owner Ed, and his girlfriend. Ed also owned a local pizzeria/restaurant where we got into some Tanqueray gin for dessert. I had just popped in to say adios before I hit the road to Mendoza but Ed set me up with a couple rounds on the house while I kept his gal company. He had promised me a taxi would pick me up at the front door first thing in the morning so I tucked my drunken ass in to bed some time shortly after last call.

Morning came, and so did the hangover...always a great way to start a long day on the road; the ride over the mountains, and border to Argentina was supposed to be about 5 hours away, and one of the most scenic rides on the continent. Not to my surprise, my taxi did not show up. It was a pretty touristy neighborhood so I didn't have to wander too many blocks dragging my bag over cobblestone before I could flag a hack down. I arrived at the bus station on time and the bus looked better than many others I had been on. I was first to board but I knew I would pay for my promptness as I watched my bag get buried behind all the others.

I decided to amuse myself with one of my favorite pastimes; people watching. As my travel mates boarded the bus I noticed two older Dutch chaps who were wearing matching Capri pants. Who was I to be the fashion critic? A cute young gal slid into the window seat beside me without giving me a second glance...so much for my mojo, but honestly I could have been her grandfather. She immediately began to play on her mobile device. I thought I'd play hard to get but she obviously won the game, since she never looked up, or uttered a word to me the whole trip. Kids!

I managed to nod off a few times before we got into the hills. The hills eventually became mountains. This is the Continental Divide, the Andes Mountains that run the entire length of the South American Continent and are the border/dividing line between Chile and Argentina. The mountains are rugged, colorful, and beautiful. I looked at one in particular out my window that kind of looked like a carton of Neapolitan ice cream cut in half. The bus started up the steep ascent; some of the peaks are over 20,000 feet and this is the only road, with a mountain pass between the two countries. The road is often impassible in the winter months because of the snow.

There was one mountain we climbed where I could see at least a dozen switchbacks going all the way up the mountainside. The huge trucks had the appearance of a Matchbox set mounted on the toy store wall. My ears popped continually, and I could feel the pressure of the change in altitude. The border between the two countries is right up among the mountain peaks, but in a barren valley. There is completely no vegetation around making the area look like a lunar landscape. The customs building is the only structure you can see for miles. Customs and Immigration was a joke and no surprise to me; we waited for quite some time in line outside the building, then we got off the bus and walked inside, only to wait for our bus to come in the building with us.

First we lined up, and then were eventually cleared for immigration. Then we got back on the bus. We drove about 100 feet and were told to get off again for a baggage check. They took every piece of luggage off the bus and had us stand in front of our bags. A Customs guy came around to us individually and he actually asked me if I had any Produce or Cocaine. I wondered if anyone ever said yes to the latter. After we cleared customs and headed out from the checkpoint I could see the road we came up on the mountain, it looked like a giant strand of black ribbon that someone had tossed down the mountain side.

We were still up in the mountain pass when we came around a corner where all traffic ahead of us was stopped. No traffic was coming the other way either so we knew something was wrong. So, there we sat for an hour with no explanation from anyone whatsoever. The movies on the bus were in Spanish and getting on my nerves; I could see the smokers on the bus were having symptoms of withdrawal. The bus driver would not let us off the bus but he got out to see what was going on. This was all it took for the smokers to rush the doors and force them open. The driver started screaming at them but everyone else followed suit and got off the bus. We had been on the bus at least 4 hours at this point, thank God for the bathroom on board.

Other vehicle drivers and passengers had been walking up the road to see what was going on ahead of us but I hung around near the bus just stretching my legs. I overheard people saying there was a landslide up ahead so I had to go see for myself. Around the bend and up the road about 20 vehicles ahead of us a large chunk of the mountain side had slid down over the road as a result of the heavy rain earlier. It didn't look like much considering the size of the mountain, just a notch out of the side, but enough to block the road. The real mess was the 4 feet of mud that slid right across the road and over the edge, down into the valley. There was a pick-up truck buried up to its doors, up off the ground and resting against the guard rail. The railing was the only thing that stopped the truck from getting swept right off the mountainside. I don't know if the truck tried to drive through the mud or it just got swept up in it. Actually, there were 4 separate slides, all visible within about a half a kilometer of road.

So, what does one do up in the middle of the mountains when 4 feet of mud cover the road and make it impassable? You sit, and wait. I heard someone say they were sending up some heavy machinery to clean up the mess. Traffic was backed up for miles but no one was turning around. I guess you don't have much choice when it is the only road available to get through the mountains and from one country to the other. So, we waited, and waited.

Another couple of hours passed and I saw a couple of backhoes on trailers being escorted to the scene. This was the "heavy equipment." No bulldozers or earthmovers, just the normal sized backhoes you'd see on any construction site. So, we waited, and waited. The bus driver said they'd have it cleaned up in an hour....right! After about 4 hours of waiting we were finally able to move on. As it turns out we weren't all that far from Mendoza, thank goodness; I was starving and the food supply ran out hours earlier! I hate arriving in any new town at night but I was now 5 hours late, arriving at about 10pm. A taxi took me into the area I wanted to stay but I had to pound the pavement, going from place to place looking for somewhere to sleep. I had to settle on a decent hotel that was about 3 times my budget, but by that time it was about 1130 at night, I was hungry, and completely wiped out.

"Mendoza is the Malbec capital of Argentina; that is just Wine by me!"

Tale of the Dragon

Smoky Mountains, Tennessee & North Carolina

"Too often . . . .I would hear men boast of the miles covered that day, rarely of what they had seen."
— Louis L'Amour

The Yacht Club

My buddy Chris and I jumped on our Harleys and headed over to Detroit in the afternoon to meet Tim and Devon, who had snuck out of work early for the day. We met the guys near their workplace in the parking lot of a bar called the Yacht club. The usual greetings and pleasantries were exchanged along with a few insults directed at each other to set the mood for the trip. A group decision was made to get right on the road and stop for a bite later, so I ran into the bar to use the bathroom. When I returned I told the boys there were naked women in the bar, all the female wait staff were wearing bikinis; another group decision was made to start the trip after a quick beer in the bar first!

I-75 at 80

We hit the big cement slab and wound our two wheelers up to speeds of 70 to 80 mph as we headed south looking for sunshine, and ultimately "The Tail of the Dragon" in the Smoky Mountains, North Carolina. For those who are unaware, the "Dragon's Tail" is a mountain road with 318 curves in 11 miles, running through Tennessee and North Carolina. It is one of the most challenging rides in North America for motorcycle and sports car enthusiasts alike. The sun tried to break out a couple times but some scattered showers eventually forced us into a gas station to gear up in our rain gear. It was a good call by Tim since the sky opened up shortly after messing up the nice shiny bikes that all three of other guys had. As usual the ride down 75 was boring and fairly uneventful.

Newport and Smart Phones

About 5 hours of hard driving put us over the Kentucky border and in the cities of Covington/Newport. We pulled into an "Extended Stay" hotel that Timmy had scoped out on the net. Booking in was left to Tim and I, Chris and Devon thought they should scope out the local bar scene. Tim had been previously quoted a room price of 80 bucks, but the best the front desk clerk would do was $110 for me at the government rate. As Tim and I discussed it a trucker guy came out of the hotel and told us we should book online with "Hotwire" since he just got a room for 80 bucks! Go figure. Sooooo, Tim got on his iphone and booked us in online. Unbelievable, you can stand in the parking lot and get a room cheaper online than walking in and booking one at the front desk!!! What has this world come to?

Covington is right across the river from Cincinnati, Ohio and Newport is nestled along side it. We jumped into a cab to get dinner in Newport, then check out the local bar scene. We sucked back some giant 1 liter beers at a German beer garden, and then moved on to restaurant/bar for some pub grub. Every time we sat down somewhere the three (*much*) younger guys would break out the iphones making me feel old (*even though I have the same phone....generational thing I guess*). Newport is a historic town on the river where they have revamped their waterfront with lots of cool restaurants and bars. We sampled a few places trying to keep the reigns on Chris, who was determined to include the rest of us in "his mission" to get wasted. More drinking, the usual guy insults and ogling very tall young women carried us through the night.

One luxury of our boys' only trips is that insults, burps and farts are pretty well expected, and accepted. We had a long day of riding ahead of us on Friday, so we (*except for Chris*) thought we'd shut it down around 1am. Chris opted for some "White Castle" burger on the walk back home.

Two Sisters Chalet

Friday was another day of hard riding, but at least the scenery got a little better in southern Kentucky, and in Tennessee. Another 5 hours or so got us to Maryville, North Carolina which is pretty close to the northern edge of Great Smoky Mountains National Park. This was our pit stop to get groceries for our night at the Chalet Tim had booked on line. Devon put the pressure on me to come up with some kind of appetizer, the boys grabbed some steaks and baked potatoes and pre-packaged Caesar salad for dinner. For the appetizers I got us a pile of shrimp, and some rolled cheese with prosciutto to put on crackers with red pepper jelly. Throw in some chips, nuts, pretzels, beer and whiskey and we were all set for the night. Some creative packing was required to strap all the stuff on to our bikes!

We had a ways to go to find our chalet that was actually up in the Smokies somewhere. The road taking us there was a pleasant surprise and a great warm up for the "Tail of the Dragon" ride. Tim actually went off the road once, but in fairness to him he was trying to look at his GPS, and addresses, while negotiating the winding, and curvy road. He eventually stopped at an old train bridge in the middle of nowhere saying that his GPS showed we were there. We had to rely on old fashioned methods and look for the address manually. Finally, Tim threw out the anchor and wheeled into a driveway taking us to the Two Sisters chalet. It was a pristine setting; the chalet was situated at the end of a long winding driveway that went over a bridge covered stream. The chalet was really a multi level three/four bedroom house with all the amenities including a hot tub.

While unpacking and snooping around the place we found that there were two barbecues, but none with propane, or charcoal. The nearest town was several miles away. I assured the boys I could make some charcoal with the right wood and sent Chris on a scavenger hunt. I was able to use a couple small logs from the fireplace stash. The three other guys all bought cigars but no one had a match to light them or start the fire, and the kitchen stove was electric. Devon was impressed; I made charcoal and did the steaks and taters up just right; oops, seems someone forgot butter for the taters. A little bit of some kind of liquid, spray butter from the cupboard helped. The boys decided they had to wash the bikes down while I made charcoal and Tim even washed mine, it was the first time since I did it the previous fall. I have to admit, it looked pretty when he was done. If the other guys spent as much time riding, as they do washing and gawking at their bikes they'd have thousands of miles on them!

Hillbillies and Gunfire

Jack Daniels came to visit after dinner and Tim brought out his pistol while we sat in the driveway sipping on our cocktails. I thought I'd take the first shot and lined up a beer can as a target. The shot rang out loud and echoed through the valley. We were all shocked and even Tim's jaw dropped. One of the hillbilly neighbors who was out riding his tractor stopped, and came walking over to our place. The boys thought we were getting kicked out for sure; well, at least we got to eat dinner first. The neighbor came over with a bottle of Wild Turkey, and a jar of pickle juice in hand; he introduced himself as "George," in a thick southern drawl. He made no mention of the gun shot and quickly accepted our offer to take a seat, and to share some cocktails.

George explained to us that Bourbon dehydrates you and the pickle juice rehydrates you, so you just chase the Bourbon with the pickle juice!

George told us all about the area, and he proceeded to get shit-faced with us. Somehow he glorified the idea of riding the Tail of the Dragon at night, and in the dark; it was only a few minutes away, Tim and Devon decided to go. I knew better but couldn't talk the boys out of it. Chris and I stayed put and entertained George. Bridgette, the owner of the chalet popped by to welcome us but she didn't stay for long. I got the impression her and George had some history. After some drinking and chatting, George said it was quite ok to shoot off guns in the hills where we were, especially if one of the abundant wild hogs in the area comes into your yard. Chris became good buddies with George, joining him in his Bourbon and pickle juice duet. He even picked up some of George's southern drawl. Tim and Devon later came back safe and sound and we all retired well hydrated, dreaming of spending the next day on the Tail of the Dragon.

The Dragon and the Skyway

We couldn't have timed our entrance to the Dragon any better since there was no one in front of us, and Tim was able to set the pace. It is difficult to describe this road to anyone who hasn't seen, or been on it. Try to imagine taking a 50 ft spool of black ribbon, unwinding it in your hands, and then tossing it out across your lawn. Now factor in some mountain terrain and you have "The Dragon"; 318 curves in 11 miles. There curves with dips, and switchbacks going up, and down hill. All of this is on a two lane road where there are hundreds of other cars and motorcycles going in various speeds in both directions. Guys on crotch rockets pass you like you're standing still, leaning so far over they have their knee on the pavement. It is great fun, but also challenging, and if you take your eyes off the road you will die. We came upon one "accident scene," where a Harley and a sport bike crashed head on, sending one of them off the road and down ravine. We later heard there were two bad accidents that day, one being fatal.

Thrills and spills are celebrated, and put on display at "Deals Gap," a "motorcycle resort" at the unofficial half way point of "The Dragon." Besides food, gas, beverages, and souvenirs, there is a tree of shame in the parking lot where various parts of crashed motorcycles hang in the tree on display. There is no shortage of shame hanging on the tree. I believe that some people just shouldn't be riding the Dragon: we were looking at a "Gold Wing" with fresh damage to one of the saddle bags; he had obviously gone down earlier that day. We later saw this same bike pulling out of Deals Gap with another Gold Wing; it fell over on the steep driveway at the edge of the road. I'm sure the spill was very embarrassing for the rider and I had to question their skill level.

We rode "The Dragon" up and down, and all around. Breakfast and t-shirts were bought at Deals Gap, and the boys did some gawking at all the different bikes. We also rode "The Little Dragon," (*the bottom half*) where we pulled over to watch some white water rafters negotiating the swollen river. The road hugs, and winds along the river making for some nice curves and great scenery. The "Cherohala Skyway" was on the way back home for the boys so we headed on up; this road runs from the river gorges to the mountain ridges, and back towards Maryville where we started from. Tim and I had done some of these roads before, but they are always enjoyable no matter how many times you ride them. Chris and Devon were noticeably smiling from ear to ear. Chris mentioned how "The Tail" honed his riding skills.

I said goodbye to the boys in Maryville, but they continued on to Cincinnati, another 5 hours away. Some people have to work for a living and had to get home, but I chilled out in Maryville and continued my southern adventure at a pace more befitting to a retiree. The boys partied in Cinci that night, and just had to let me know at 3am that they found a watering hole they liked. They got to enjoy a hangover ride back to Detroit and Windsor the next day, getting home in time for dinner.

"This is only one tale of "The Dragon"

Freebird

"When we get out of the glass bottle of our ego and when we escape like the squirrels in the cage of our personality and get into the forest again, we shall shiver with cold and fright. But things will happen to us so that we don't know ourselves. Cool, unlying life will rush in."

– D. H. Lawrence

Little River Road

I woke up and hit the road at leisure after saying bye-bye to the boys in Maryville, North Carolina the previous night. I had been motorcycle riding with my buddies Chris, Tim, and Devon for the three days prior from Windsor/Detroit to the Smoky Mountains. Our destination had been the motorcyclists dream road, The Tail of the Dragon....318 curves in 11 miles. We also took in the Cherahola Skyway before they headed for Cincinnati and I bedded down for the night to rest up for my more leisurely ride home. Some people still have to work for living, poor bastards.

I didn't even look at the map until the morning and made my decision to head east in the Smokies along the Blue Ridge Parkway to Asheville, North Carolina. Heading out of Maryville to Cherokee, North Carolina I took a scenic short cut called the Little River Road. As soon as I got on this road I knew I was in for a morning treat. It started with a narrow bridge that crossed over a rushing, white water river. The road immediately grabbed and followed the edge of the river; always a treat to ride since no river ever runs a straight line or level.

I had stopped for breakfast so it was later in the morning, but the sun was still low in the sky creating some great shadows through the tree canopies and on to the shiny black road. The water in the rushing and gushing river sparkled and glittered like diamonds in the dappled sunlight. There was barely any other traffic on the road so I just cruised at my own pace. It was still and quiet except for my exhaust pipes that echoed off the shear rock cliff that was on my right side. I couldn't hear the sound of the rushing water but did notice the sporadic bursts of some kind of bright white flowers that stood out against the dark green foliage on the river banks. The cool morning air held the scent of the fresh blossoms that smelled like jasmine.

Hundreds of butterflies fluttered above the road and in and out of the shrubbery and along the river. There were yellow and black ones, and blue and black ones. The little guys looked like Christmas light bulbs being turned on and off as they darted in and out of the sunlight and shadows from the trees. One of them got caught in the dead air zone between me and the windshield; he just floated there like he was suspended in time, then a gust of wind swept him away. A chipmunk scampered across the road in front of me. The weather was perfect, a bit hot in the sun but slightly cool in the shade. I loved the contrast.

Taking Flight

The Little River Road ended at the scenic parkway that runs from Gatlinburg, Tennessee to Cherokee, and North Carolina directly through the middle of the Great Smoky Mountain National Park. I've travelled this route several times over the years but you can never tire of it. It's not as winding as the Dragon Tail since the curves are easier and more graceful. There are some great switchbacks though, and one actual 360 degree loop where you go through a tunnel and then loop around over the top of it on the same road. I was enjoying the ride as usual until I got held up for at least a half hour in a construction zone.

Then, I was rewarded for my long delay by the one of my best mountain rides ever! After the construction zone the mountain road started to fade down hill. I was the first vehicle out of the gate so there was no one in front of me. I started to cruise downhill in the 45mph zone at about 50. The curves were quite manageable at that speed and I noticed my speed was holding steady while cruising down the mountain. I pulled the clutch all the way in cutting power to the engine and I just coasted. I cleared my ears from the change in altitude and caught the sound of silence. All I could hear was the wind rushing over my ears. The broken rays of the sun coming through the tree canopies danced off my face when I looked up to find the sky. I could smell the white flowers in the air again and more butterflies joined me in their sun dance.

I noticed I was smiling from ear to ear, and I kicked the gear shifter into neutral. Then I took flight. I stretched my arms straight out to my sides, steering the bike with my knees and I flew just like a bird. I just tilted my wings a bit in the bends and I flew down the mountain like that for about three miles. I was almost giddy as I felt goose bumps creeping over me. What can I say.....it was incredible, amazing, and just awesome!!! It may sound corny but at that moment I just felt at peace and one with the universe. I eventually had to put the bike back in gear and put my hands back on the handle bars to negotiate the remainder of the roadway.

"It was a defining moment in my life; and for that moment, I was as free as a bird!"

North and South

Michigan State, U.S.A.

"A good traveler has no fixed plans and is not intent on arriving."
– Lao Tzu

The Labor Day holiday weekend was fast approaching, and I was overdue for another bike trip before the summer weathered away. My girlfriend Cathryn was itching to come with me for two reasons: first, she loves riding on the back of my Harley, and she was anxious to see how she fared on a long road trip. Second, and most importantly to her, she wanted to show off her new "Harley Davidson" attire, and perhaps get the chance to accessorize some more while on the trip. The plan was to head across the border into Michigan, and catch a few scenic rides in the state between Lakes Huron, and Michigan.

We headed out Friday morning, sleeping in a bit to let the morning traffic thin out ahead of us. The temperature was already in the 90's as I packed up the bike. I had traveled alone on the bike "B.C." *(Before Cathryn)*, so I now had to give up one saddle bag, and half my luggage space to her. She met the packing challenge with room to spare, but I noted she wasn't too thrilled about leaving her hair dryer behind. Hmm, hair dryer, or extra room for new clothes? It was a tough choice for her maiden voyage on two wheels. I really didn't mind bringing her along since she looked pretty hot with her curly blonde hair sticking out of her helmet and just the right amount of cleavage showing out of her tank top.

We crossed the Windsor/Detroit border with very little traffic, nice treat considering the combined heat of the day, along with the bike's engine. The Customs agent was actually pleasant; he corrected my mistake when I said we were touring the "Upper Peninsula." For those others out there who are geographically challenged Detroit, Michigan is actually north of Windsor, Ontario. So, you actually go north, into a country that is south of us on the map! I'm sure most of you non-bikers are also ignorant to the fact that motorcycles are not allowed in the tunnel so the "Ambassador Bridge" is the only biking option when crossing the border *(the law changed 20 something years ago for safety reasons).*

I usually stick to the back roads on my bike when I have no set agenda but the only way to sensibly get out of Detroit is by freeway. We had the day to kill, with the intentions to hook up with some friends in Milford Michigan later in the evening. I figured the Irish Hills could provide a few hours of scenic riding so I headed out I-94 west to the Saline exit where you can pick up U.S. 12 *(Michigan Ave)*. This is also called the "Chicago road" since it was once the only way there from Detroit, before the Interstate highways were built. I prefer the winding two laners that almost always provide a better view and a more enjoyable ride. I hadn't been out that way in at least 30 years, when I rode with the "Blue Knights*" (police motorcycle club)*, or went skydiving in Tecumseh, Michigan. The town of Clinton looked familiar since it is where we used to turn off for Tecumseh. Another advantage of travelling the back roads of America is seeing the scenic little towns with turn of the century building, and the individual character, that just doesn't compare in the city. One magnificent Victorian mansion got a "Wow" in harmony, from both C and I.

I didn't have a radio on my bike at that time, but the road and scenery usually provided me with all the entertainment I ever needed. Cathryn didn't seem to mind either since she had the best seat on the bike, you just get to sit back and enjoy the sights, and ride. It was a great day for riding since the heat subsided a bit outside the city and the air conditioning is always on at 50 mph on the bike. I think the Irish Hills area starts somewhere after Clinton; it is noticeable with a hillier, and more forested landscape. There are also dozens of little lakes scattered throughout the area, kind of like cottage country in the Muskoka area of Ontario. We stayed right on U.S. 12 to Cement City or an intersection called, "Artesian Wells," where the "Town and Country" Harley dealership is located. An excellent restaurant right next door provided us with a couple ice cold beers, and the best chicken quesadilla I've ever had!

A couple beers, lunch, and a butt rest was enough to work up a shopping appetite for Cathryn, so off to the Harley store we went. Anyone who knows anything about Harley Davidson will know that they make more money on their merchandizing than they do on motorcycles. They have also taken advantage of a woman's appetite for shopping and accessorizing, and that section of the store is now about 3 times larger than the men's; go figure.

While C was busy trying on clothes, I was busy with the map planning the next leg of our leisurely jaunt through the Irish Hills. I was looking for a route north and eventually back east to Milford where we would overnight at Tim and Patty's place. While I was looking at the map another Harley guy asked if I was lost. When I told him what I was looking for he suggested some back roads I'd like, to get me where I wanted to go. I lost him after about the first three roads; *(not even on the map)* he said we could just follow him if we liked. "What the hey," is what I say. I was shocked when Cathryn came out of the store empty handed, but I knew the trip wasn't over yet.

The guy's *(never did catch his name)* bike was parked right beside mine in the lot. It was a 1978 H.D. Low Rider with lots of miles, and visible wear on it. He smiled as he told me about it, so as long as he was happy, life was good. We continued west to Moscow and took the Moscow road north; it was my kind of road. Immediately the road narrowed, and trees on both side formed a cooling canopy over our heads. The pavement dipped and weaved through the countryside, sprinkled with farms and swampland.

Moscow road then turned into Deering road; a fitting name since two Whitetails *(Deer)* darted into the road about a hundred feet ahead of our escort. Buddy had enough room to avoid them, but it definitely made my heart skip a beat.

Cathryn and I had just stopped talking about the Deer when I saw what I thought was a large rock in the middle of the road. It was actually a big turtle lumbering across the road to the creek nearby. It is great to see nature when you're riding, but its better when it's not on the road in front of you. We meandered down some other country roads, some without names but well worth the ride. This guy definitely knew where he was going, he said he had grown up around there, but was now living in Arkansas. I think it was about an hour or so when he pulled over into a gas station and pointed to I 96, the route I wanted to Milford. Cool! Thanks to the unknown biker escort, it was a great ride! Note to the unknown biker: Your old hawg burns oil and it don't taste too good from behind.

Freeway riding is never scenic and almost always boring with the exception you have to keep your wits about you when everyone is doing at least 70 mph and changing lanes. We took the highway to Brighton and stopped at a Myers to pick up some wine for Tim and Patti's place. It always pisses me off when shopping in the states since you can get booze for half of the price it is in Canada. Ok, I do smile at the time, when I'm saving money. Tim called to check on our progress and asked me to pick up a 100 lb bag of charcoal...Asshole! *(Bike humor)*.

We made it to Milford and our friends' residence right at 5pm as planned but Tim and Patti had not made it home yet. Thank God for cell phones, keypad garage door openers; and Tim's supply of cold beer! Tim soon arrived home from work with Patti and the girls arriving shortly after. Cathryn learned what a hot and sticky day on the bike does to you and welcomed a hose down in the shower. I settled on a couple more beers. It was now dinner time and Tim thought it was way too hot to even think about lighting up the Q. We all agreed and went out for dinner.

For dessert Tim and Patti took us to their country club for cocktails and a swim, perfect activities given the mood and weather. It was a bit hot for the hot tub but it felt good on my aging bones and my tender ass after a full day of riding. Of course the cocktails felt good too, they always taste better when someone else is buying them! The pool felt great and Uncle Ed attempted to teach Alex how to dive without plugging her nose. I didn't master the feat till I was twelve I think, so I appreciated her dilemma. Maybe I should have learned from her and plugged my ears; they always get plugged up with water.

We finished off the evening back at the house with more drinks, some chatting, and some laughs. Cathryn was a hit with Elizabeth and Alex; she showed them how to do a French manicure on their nails. Alex offered up her bedroom to Cathryn and I and we all retired at a reasonable hour since we had some more riding planned for the morning. Some more friends, Devon and Chella were to be joining us for a ride up to Bay City, Michigan.

The morning came with only a two Tylenol hangover. The pills and breakfast took care of the headache. The heat outside was another story; it had to be 95 by 10am, with the humidex making it about 149! I was soaked right through my shirt by the time the Devon and Chella arrived, late I might add. People with kids, I just can't comprehend. We all mounted our iron horses, three completely different machines; Tim was on a Yamaha, Devon on a Beemer, and me on my hawg. Oh yeah, the girls were coming along too. We headed out on the Milford road; what a great road to start the day off, winding and curvy, tree canopies, scenic little towns like Holly, just awesome!

Timmy took the lead, taking us on the back roads all the way to Bay City where we had lunch at a restaurant on the water. It had a great patio, but it seemed the rain had followed us there and then chased us inside the restaurant. It wasn't a meal to brag about but it filled the void. The stop wasn't a complete waste; the restaurant had a great wine store in it with some amazing bargains. I scored two bottles of a California cab for 10 bucks! Only in the U.S.A. The rain had stopped so we said our goodbyes to our friends who were returning home, while C and I headed west toward Lake Michigan.

I chose U.S. 10 which goes northwest right across the fingers part of the mitt *(Michigan talk)*. It is mostly freeway until about halfway, where it scales down. We decided to head for Cadillac, Michigan for the evening. Sometimes when you're on two wheels, you get to a point where you just don't feel like riding anymore; this was one of those days. We settled in at the hotel, and then walked across the parking lot to an authentic Mexican restaurant. I ordered a T-bone steak; cravings, you know how they are. The margaritas were the drink special and they came in fishbowls, just perfect! A couple of those and a couple bottles of the wine we bought made for a good nights sleep.

Sunday was a beautiful day, the sun was shining and the heat had died down. We decided to see Traverse City and headed north. Traverse City looks like any other city, until you head to the water where it takes on its own personality. Being a holiday weekend, there were throngs of people along the shores of the upper part of Lake Michigan. The city has a beautiful waterfront with beaches, parkland, and marinas. We were only there for a drive through, so we followed the waterfront out of town where the scenic Hwy 22 starts. The road follows the waters edge along the western arm of Grand Traverse Bay. There's always something spectacular about riding along the water; its color perhaps, or the different types and sizes of boats, or just the natural beauty of it all.

We followed 22 north for awhile, impressed by the beautiful homes and cottages. I spotted a winery sign along the road and wheeled into the Black Star Winery for a taste and looks see. It was a huge place that could have compared with some of the Estates I saw in the Sonoma Valley in California. This place was an Inn, riding stable, winery, cheese factory, and restaurant all set in a beautiful valley surrounded by grape vines and well manicured gardens. We scored a lovely chardonnay and a chunk of cheese for a treat later on. Further on down the road we ran across many more wineries but we had to pass them buy *(how sad)*.

At Sutton's Bay another road allows you to cut across the tip of land that continues up to Northport. Lake Leelanau is about half way across and was a good scenic spot for a lunch stop. It was too bad the town was voted one of America's best on Good Morning America since it was packed with more tourists than normal making it almost impossible to get lunch. The staff at more than one restaurant was completely frazzled. It was 130pm and we couldn't get into any of the sit down places so we settled on a slice and a soda at a variety store/deli.

Heading west again we soon came to Hwy 22 again and we went south along the lake towards Sleeping Bear Dunes National Lakeshore. I had read and been told this was a must see area with the sand dunes rising 700 feet above Lake Michigan. Well, maybe next time, the sites were so packed with tourists the rangers had to block access and shut the roads down because of traffic jams. Onward we went taking in some lake views and some nice winding roads but for the most part the scenery consisted of many, many trees. We did find a scenic vantage point on the lake at Point Betsie where there is a historic lighthouse. Muskegon was a little out of reach for the day so we decided to call it a day in Manistee.

We followed signs for the old town and tried a beautiful old restored Inn on the main drag. They were full up as well as the next place down the road. Three was our lucky number and the Riverside motel/marina gave up their last room to us. The place looked pretty clean but it wasn't cheap; it was a holiday weekend!

The clerk was overly friendly and helpful, and invited us to their year end bash out back of the motel. Our room was typical of the old road side motels but very clean. I cracked the chardonnay and we hit the showers. Just then the sky opened up and I could see sideways rain, outside the window. Cathryn had to run out and rescue her Oyster crackers she left sitting on the bike. Seems our timing was perfect in missing the rain, once again.

A bottle of wine, a chunk of cheese, some crackers, and two showers later, the rain slowed to a light drizzle; we decided to throw on our rain coats, and go for a walk to look for a proper dinner. Just for the hell of it we poked our heads around the corner of the motel to check out the party. A guy *(the owner)* hollered at us to step up and grab a plate, the steaks were on! He told us the last thing we should be was shy and we should help ourselves to the New York strip steaks, fries, salads, and cold beer. Well, Cathryn and I are not shy so we obliged. I even found a bottle of Canadian whiskey to crack open after my two steaks with fixins and the beer filled me up. Not wanting to refuse the generous hospitality we even took drinks back to the room. It seems the hotel puts on this shindig every year on Labor Day, boy did we luck out!

The rain and winds put an end to the entertainment and eventually the party so we ran out of booze. Cathryn seemed like the perfect candidate to scrounge us up another round of drinks from the owner who was out cleaning up after the party. The booze was gone but he said his brother in law "Jimmy" would drive her to the party store since it was too nasty to walk the few blocks. Unbeknownst to me she climbed in the truck with Jimmy; his smile with a few teeth missing must have won her trust. She was a little uneasy by all the rifles hanging in the window and asked about all the spot lights on top. Jimmy said they were for Deer "watching," apparently they just watch the Deer and the rifles are for show *(lol)*. Like the trooper she is, Cathryn showed up back at the room with more wine and a story about her ride with "Jimmy."

Monday morning was a shocker; the temperature had dropped about 40 degrees and it was still overcast, but at least it wasn't raining. We were hoping to take in Silver Lake and White Sands on the way home but after riding in the 55 to 60 degree weather for awhile we just made the beeline for home. Cathryn put on every piece of clothes she had but we still needed to make a stop at Wal-Mart, so she could add a layer. She couldn't bend her legs or arms but she never complained, a true biker bitch! Cold is better than wet but it takes its toll on you after awhile. Going 70 to 80mph on the Interstate doesn't help to warm things at all. Needless to say the trip from Muskegon, through Grand Rapids and home was not much fun, such is biking some times. We covered about 800 miles in the four days but took in some great sights from Lake Huron to Lake Michigan. Cathryn passed the long haul test and we both look forward to our next adventure. Geez, she didn't get to buy any new H.D. clothes.

"You don't have to go far for new adventures...just go!"

The Train & the Tower

Toronto, Ontario

*"It is easy to differentiate between a traveler and non-traveler.
One is open-minded, accepting, humble, gracious, imaginative,
spontaneous and fun loving. The other is neither."*

– Doris Chow

The Train

I've traveled to various parts of the world in search of unique places, people, and even adventure but I was recently reminded you don't have to wander too far from home to find these things. Far too often we all take for granted places that are close to home and that can tease your imagination, or titillate your travel senses. I've been to Toronto, Ontario many times over the years for a number of reasons but it was only on a recent trip that I fully appreciated the capital city of Ontario for its vibrancy, culture, and a truly fun place to be.

This trip was initiated by my purchase of two tickets to the latest travelling Cirque du Soleil show, "Totem." For those who don't know, a Cirque show is a sensual injection of sorts; it is technically a circus without animals that originated in Montreal, Quebec about 20 years ago. The performers are the best of the best, working with creative and colorful costumes, orchestrated music and lighting. They now have permanent shows all over the world, but a new travelling show comes to Toronto each year. I have seen shows there, in Las Vegas, Detroit, and Windsor. Each show is unique and never disappointing.

My home is in the City of Windsor, in Ontario, called "The Asshole" of Canada by some, for its bottom of the country location, and the way we are sometimes perceived by the folks

149

north of London. Toronto is about 3-1/2 hours up the highway or railway from Windsor, depending on whether you like to drive or let someone else do it for you. My bff *(Cathryn)* and I decided to take advantage of a half fare ticket sale and ride the iron horse to "Hog Town." Toronto's had many nicknames over the years but most of us just refer to it as "T.O." If you are a true Torontonian you can say the name all in one syllable….like…"Tranh."

I hadn't taken the train to Toronto in at least 20 years but it does have advantages if you want to relax, read, or play on the internet with your wireless device. If you are staying downtown you have the further advantage of Union Station that is close to many good hotels and you don't have to pay ridiculous parking fees. Our baggage proved to be a bit of an obstacle *(for me)* since I was the pack mule carrying luggage for two. Cathryn had the displeasure of tearing her Achilles tendon a few days before we left, so she had to hobble around on crutches. She just didn't seem to get a handle on how to properly operate her extra set of legs, but she got special treatment and extra help boarding the train. Nobody helped poor me though, carrying two suitcases, a shoulder bag, and her purse!

Downtown

I don't think that trains have changed much in the last 20 years, but the ride seemed a lot smoother without that clickity-clack racket you used to get before they installed seamless tracks. The ride seemed a lot quicker too, maybe it was my chatty female companion, or the luxury of being able to look at pictures and surf the net on my lap top; it's still legal to text and ride on the train. We were in Toronto before we knew it, and a cheap cab ride landed us at the Delta Chelsea where a friend had secured us a family and friend's rate that didn't cost me an arm and a leg. It's an upscale hotel centrally located in the heart of downtown.

I was a little surprised to see an actual balcony with our room; most high rise hotels these days bolt the windows shut to keep their guests from jumping, and not paying their bills. Standing out on the balcony and looking out over the city you would never know we were in a recession with all the building going on. There always seems to be something getting torn down, with something bigger being built in its place in Toronto. Right across the street they were building the highest condo complex in the country. You can own your own cement cubicle there for a measly 1.3 million dollars. I was equally impressed with the view on the balcony when I noticed Cathryn was standing beside me completely naked *(just a little thing she likes to do)* .When I regained my senses I spotted the "Elephant & Castle" pub down below; we decided it was high time for a beer.

A few pints at the pub brought on a hunger so we discussed our dinner options. I think we may have had some mussels to hold us over and if we did they weren't notable enough to remember. Cathryn had a few places in mind and she was kind of playing tour guide for me. I've never been one to enlist favorites so I had no preferences from any of my prior visits to the city. C suggested the "Ciao Wine Bar" in Yorkville, so away we went. I don't recall ever looking at a tourist map of Toronto, and I never really appreciated the distinctly different neighborhoods in the downtown core. Yorkville is just north of Queens Park, and can easily be called an upscale area with trendy shops, and fancy restaurants.

Yorkville

One review I read called "Ciao Wine Bar" a cross between South Beach and Italy, a pretty extreme contrast I think. Anyhoo, we were a bit late in the evening for dinner but that seems to be the norm in the big city. The wine list was a bit scattered....they tried to bridge the gap between California and Italy I think. It was a bit pricey for our tastes but I found a great Italian syrah for less than my monthly pension cheque. I do know a bit about wine and I was a quite intrigued by my find; Syrah's are more common in France and Australia. We decided to carb up, and both ordered pasta dishes. My Spaghetti Carbonara was just perfect but Cathryn thought her gnocchi was too dry and she traded it in for the same dish as me. The kitchen whipped it up pronto just for her, accepting her for the princess she truly is.

While in Yorkville, Cathryn said I had to check out the view from the roof top bar at the Park Hyatt, around the corner from the restaurant. I felt like I should have taken my shoes off when entering the lobby of this place, pretty swanky to say the least! C warned me it was about $12 for a beer or mixed drink, hell the cab ride was cheaper! We made out in the elevator just because we could, then exited on the top floor *(I have no idea how many floors there are)*. It was only about 45 or 50 degrees outside with a light wind; this made it easy to find a ringside seat to the best view I've ever had of Toronto. We sat right up against the glass railing where we could see Queens Park, and the CN Tower further south. The tower was lit up like a giant rocket, and the city lights sparkled like broken glass scattered across the pavement. To keep customers on the chilly roof top the hotel had elaborate gas heaters installed, and hanging above our heads. They also supplied fuzzy blankets, something I have never seen anywhere before.

I have to say the view and the ambiance was impressive, romantic, and a unique experience! Add to that a celebrity sighting for the complete Toronto experience; I noted a couple of gentlemen in formal, military style attire at the bar inside. They escorted some women to the patio outside to show them the view and one of them said, "This is my city, it has many great things to see." I recognized him as Bill Blair, the Toronto police chief. He commands about 6,000 cops in Hog Town.

Nuit Blanche

Saturday morning we did something I don't ever recall doing; we ordered breakfast from room service. You always think of it as shitty, highly overpriced food but this was the Delta Chelsea, in Toronto! Breakfast out meant a brisk walk or a cab ride in search of a descent place, and where can you get breakfast in downtown T.O. for less than the price of a newborn black market baby? C likes to split meals so we did the eggs Benny with a couple extras and didn't even have to do dishes to cover the cost. The service was prompt, the food was good and hot, and I didn't even have to get out of my jammies. And so what if I still had bed head.

After a shit, shave, and shower it was time to walk up an appetite for lunch. C wanted to take me to "The Corned Beef House" on Adelaide. The hotel is "kind of" on Yonge Street so we walked south; well, I walked and she hobbled on her magic legs. We *(she)* were having a little trouble dodging the foot traffic on the sidewalk so we ventured into the street. Normally this would be impossible but there was a huge art festival called "Nuit Blanche" going on and Yonge Street was completely blocked off from traffic. It's much easier to take in the sights when you can walk down the middle of the street. Some of the artists were setting up; it looked a bit weird to me but "art "is weird to me. One display was two big stacks of plywood in the middle of the street with some construction barricades spiraled out like a deck of cards, and a wall of yellow caution tape strung up between light standards; yes, art!

We walked and hobbled and stretched our legs while the artists and set up people scrambled around us. The festival wasn't to start until 7pm, but then it would run right through the night to 7am. Yikes, note to self: make sure we're not out on the street too late. C wanted to show me the St. Lawrence Market so we walked over to it and plunged into the crowd. It's an impressively old, humongous covered market with a wide assortment of people, as well as food stuff. She did some cheese sampling while I inhaled a cookie and diet coke *(balancing my diet)*. The assortment of food smells confused my senses; I wasn't even hungry! The crowd consisted of a kaleidoscope of people from every corner of the world who now called Toronto home. It wasn't long before we felt we could stuff another meal into ourselves so off to the Corned Beef House we went. It is actually an old house with a pizza place in the basement, and the deli on the main floor. I was surprised the owner recognized Cathryn from her prior visit....hmm. She usually splits a Rueben but I talked her into the Montreal Smoked Meat with Swiss cheese, on marble bread, grilled... Oooooh yeah....I knew I'd convert her!

The Circus

Another cheap taxi ride got us to Cherry Street in the Docklands, near the cruise ship terminal. This hack even blew a couple red lights back to back, so I had no problem tipping him. We weren't in any hurry but I assumed he just didn't like stopping when the lights turned red. For the uninitiated, arrival on site at Cirque gives you the impression you really are at the Circus with the giant blue and yellow tents. "Cirque Du Soleil" trucks everything in that you see on site, including the big top, concessions, and lavatories. Once inside the tent, it takes on the appearance of a theatre with padded folding seats, and a custom made stage that transforms throughout the show. If you feel like giving up a week's salary you can first stop in at the "Tapis Rouge" tent where you are literally treated to a red carpet, free drinks and appetizers. Exclusive seating comes with the special ticket.

I had chosen the second row directly across the isle from the expensive seats, paying much less. They were probably the best seats I've ever had for a Cirque show, but of course some large woman, with even larger hair was sitting directly in front of Cathryn, who is somewhat vertically challenged. Sitting on both of our coats helped raise her up a bit to see over the giant Chia Pet. She thought she should have at least been entitled to one of the kiddies booster seats they were handing out. The show was amazing as usual, with everything I've come to expect from Cirque. Sitting that close you can get a better appreciation of the make-up and costumes, and the amazing physiques on some of the performers. Cathryn is now a Cirque fan.

Prior to the show and during intermission, you have to walk through the concession area where they flaunt their souvenirs and memorabilia. C saw one of the employees with a cute little hat on and just had to have one. I just laughed out loud when she said they were only 5 bucks, wrong tag honey! They're like mini clown hats that some of the performers have worn in certain shows. It obviously caught on; I saw a woman watching Cathryn model hers, then I saw the same woman again later sporting her own hat. I rarely fall victim to the overpriced goodies but for some strange reason they offered the show soundtrack and a colored program for only $20 this year. I think the last time I was there they were 20 bucks each! Good score I thought.

The Esplanade

This is twice now I've taken a taxi to the Docklands and twice I've had to walk back; there never seems to be any taxis after the show. Oh well, it was a nice evening and there was still some daylight; Cathryn said she'd tough it out on her alumalimbs and we strolled up into the historic Distillery District, then on to The Esplanade. It's a narrow tree-lined street/park, nice for strolling. Just past Mark Street and the St Lawrence Market, a few bars and restaurants appeared. "The Bier Market" called out our names, and an "Okanagan Springs Amber Ale" made its way down my pie hole quite easily. Funny, it tasted "like more." There were 100 and something different kinds of imported beers in this place, most of them on tap with a cool keg room visible through plate glass windows. I chatted with a jet-lagged couple from Switzerland for a bit at the bar just to be sociable. I tried to get some news on the Tiger (*Detroit*) game back home but pre-season hockey was more important in T.O. than play-off Baseball in the U.S.

We ordered some ridiculously overpriced, but delicious appetizer to hold us over till dinner; bacon wrapped scallops, as I was reminded upon writing this story. It was my time to choose a dinner spot and I picked the "Keg Mansion." Cathryn wasn't thrilled because we could Keg it at home but I played my trump card. On arrival, I was pleased to see that the restaurant was actually an old mansion restored and converted. We ignorantly entered without a reservation and were politely told the wait would be an hour, or more. Seating upstairs in the bar area was first come, first served so I went for a peek. The bar area looked like the trading floor of the N.Y. Stock Exchange. I did notice that the interior woodwork and the décor were beautiful. I returned to Cathryn's side with the mob near the front doors. The hostess must have seen the look of pain in C's face and she came over to tell us we'd be seated right away. It's amazing where a couple artificial limbs can get you! I think we were almost finished our desert when a couple was seated beside us, they had been ahead of us in line. We were pleasantly surprised that the menu prices were the same as at home and substantially cheaper than what we paid at the Keg in Niagara Falls.

Street Life

Our cab dropped us somewhere near our hotel on Yonge Street and we strolled amongst the crowds. There was a guy on a tall unicycle juggling lit torches, but somehow it just didn't compare to Cirque. Everyone was bundled up because of the chilly weather and they seemed quite orderly, although it wasn't even midnight yet. We decided to end our night at the Elephant & Castle once again, since it was close to home. My crippled companion got us a seat again, ahead of those waiting in line. It almost makes you want to travel with a pair of crutches all the time. A few night caps and some people watching made for a nice wrap up to the weekend.

Some final observations of hanging downtown were that it is definitely Yuppie Ville. I also noted that many of the couples were of the same sex and in many cases, gay. I had learned from my previous visit that there is a specific Gay area near the old Maple Leaf Gardens; they actually have their own flag (ya learn something new every day) that is displayed out front specific establishments. It was pretty cool that you could safely walk most streets in the downtown neighborhoods, even though I barely noticed any cops. I was also pleasantly surprised that most of our taxi fares were less than 10 bucks. There are street cars and a subway that's easily accessible if you need to venture further.

Although I enjoyed the weekend and the whole Toronto experience, I was reminded that it can still be a cold place when it comes to its people. Like any big city I guess, people don't generally talk to you unless they really have to. No nods or hellos or even eye contact for that matter. We were waiting in the train station for our departure and I noted several people wearing pink shirts for some type of Cancer Walk. I asked one woman in line with me at Cinnabon stand what the walk was for, and she completely ignored me. I repeated my question a little louder, thinking she didn't hear me; I was greeted with a look of disgust, a sarcastic and abrupt answer of "cancer walk!" Then she turned, and walked away making me feel like I had just propositioned her for sex. Such is life in the Big City.

"Even a weekend away...is getting away!"

Breeze in Belize

Caye Caulker, Belize

"Make voyages. Attempt them. There is nothing else."
                                        – Tennessee Williams

The country of Belize had always been on my list of places to see but I had heard it was more of a relaxed and romantic spot suited for couples. After travelling solo for a few years to places with a bit more "action," I decided to discover Belize with my special someone. In my research and planning of the trip I had to consider the neighboring country of Guatemala since I wanted to see some Mayan ruin sites and "Tikal" is one of the best. The country of Belize lies just south of Mexico on the Atlantic Ocean and shares a border with Guatemala. I had heard and read that Belize City was a "shit-hole" so I decided we'd spend part of our cold Canadian winter on Caye Caulker, one of the islands of Belize. Pronounced "Key Cocker" by the locals, I chose it over Ambergris Caye to the north, where it is more busy, touristy, and expensive.

Getting to Caye Caulker is a bit of an adventure in itself for the un-initiated traveler. In getting to Belize from pretty well anywhere in North America, you have to go through Miami. Direct flights from Miami take you to Belize City. Once there, you can take a puddle jumper to Caye Caulker for about $65 U.S., or take a water taxi from the port. I chose to initiate myself with the 30 minute taxi ride from the airport to the port for $25 U.S. The taxi driver knew the ferry schedules and drove like a mad man to get me there in time for the next departure. Like in most third world countries, cruising through Belize City was not very scenic and it could double for any other large Mexican or Central American city. The "shit-hole" description I had been given was quite fitting; I hate places where everyone eyeballs you like you're a child molester. The water taxi terminal was a breeze with porters whisking you and your luggage to the ticket counter and boat ($9 one way).

The water taxi was basically a large fishing boat with hard benches for seats in the cabin and two large screaming engines for propulsion. The captain sat up on the top deck and the passengers are crammed into the cabin below. There is no assigned seating and I sincerely doubt that they adhere to any limit of how many people they can carry. My research said the boat ride was 20 minutes but it was 45 to Caye Caulker. I later found that there is a jet boat that does it in 20 but it had an erratic schedule. The ride was nothing to brag about and you couldn't see much from the belly of the boat anyhow. I was mostly entertained by people watching on the boat; you could tell the locals from the tourists mostly by the tans or sun burns. I was particularly amused by the short woman beside me whose feet could not reach the floor; she was bounced off her seat every time we hit a wave and she struggled to hang on to her grocery bag while trying to keep her balance.

The Island

A big jolly black man said, "Welcoom to Key Cocker" as we docked and I stepped on to the wooden pier. The pastel colors of the buildings on the beach accented with numerous palm trees immediately caught my eye. Something told me right off I was going to like this place as my sandals met the sandy beach and I inhaled the clean tropical air. It was only a short walk to the Caye Caulker Real Estate office where I had to check in for my beach bungalow. I had booked it online for $1,100 U.S. for four weeks. Ray, the landlord showed up promptly with his golf cart and shuttled me down the road to the bungalow. "Ray" was casually dressed, fair-haired and slight in build with an Aussie accent; he gave me a quick lay-out of the town as we drove along the sandy main road that was no more than a hard packed pathway.

The road was lined on both sides with little shops, restaurants, bars, and grocery stores, as well travel agencies and places to stay. None of the buildings were any taller than the palm trees and everyone was wandering along the road in bathing suits and flip flops. I saw several other golf carts and some bicycles; Ray told me there were no paved roads and no motor vehicles allowed on the island, with the exception of construction vehicles. The island only has 3 main roads that travel its 4 mile length. Apparently the island was originally 5 miles long but the last hurricane cut it in two. If you stand on the east beach and look down a cross road you can see the west beach not too far away. I saw plenty of places to eat and drink, but only one bank and ATM on the island; it dispensed Belizean dollars *(about 50 cents U.S.)*

The island is populated with a friendly mix of locals born on the island, some Jamaican immigrants, and a large number of ex-pats from various countries throughout the world. English is the main language spoken with some Spanish and a slang type of Creole spoken by the locals. The street vendors were mostly Jamaican but they did not hassle you like they do in so many other tropical destinations. They sold the usual trinkets or souvenirs and some had little barbeques set up grilling the catch of the day for lunch. I saw signs for fresh snapper, lobster, and conch.....yum! I saw one place where lobster traps were piled high and it reminded me of Peggy's Cove in Nova Scotia.

Beach Bungalow

So what exactly do you get for $1,100 for a whole month when booking over the internet? It was pretty well what I had expected when Ray gave me the grand tour of the one room wooden bungalow. I guess it could be best described as a bachelor unit with the bathroom partitioned off but with the walls only about 6' high and not up to the ceiling. Yes, Cathryn and I later grew much closer....getting first hand knowledge of each others bowel movements. The bungalow was fully equipped with a bed and sofa, fridge and stove, T.V., and fans to keep cool. There was even free wireless internet available. I could see the beach through the window or from the porch that was equipped with chairs. Ray and Mariya's house was right on the beach and the bungalow was behind it by the road. The house was on stilts so you could also see the ocean by looking directly under it. This layout also allowed for some great ocean breezes. The temperature there is usually in the 80's, quite acceptable for a Snowbird from Canada.

Nothing to Do and All Day to Do It

I had wondered before going to a small island if I would be bored or run out of things to do since I sometimes get antsy when sitting still for too long. This didn't seem to be the case on Caye Caulker. If anyone is looking for an island getaway where you want to do nothing with all day to do it this is the place. It has to be one of the most laid back places I've ever visited. No McDonalds or name brand clothing stores, just little mom and pop run businesses. There are plenty of water related activities but of the leisurely sort....you don't hear many jet skis or see any power boats ripping up and down the beach. I was told things had slowed down with the recession limiting the number of tourists visiting the island. I had to wonder how some of the businesses managed since they were empty most of the time.

Although eating and drinking are two of my favorite travel activities, I do walk quite a bit to explore and wear off the previous meal. You can actually walk from one end of the island to the other if you so desire. There is the road that narrows to a path down to the mangroves at the south end and a place called "The Split" at the north end. There is a cool bar called "The Lazy Lizard" overlooking The Split; it is an open channel where the last hurricane ripped through, cutting the island in two. There is some beach here with great ocean breezes and that turquoise colored water that we search the world for. You can truly appreciate the view and breeze from the second level of the bar where you can sip on a cold beverage and people watch, or just do nothing. They serve food there too but we experienced mixed results with it. The Split offers the best beach on the island and it's where most sun worshippers hang out during the day.

There are a few massage tables set up in the shade if you need any of life's stresses rubbed out of your muscles. Most days a colorful, rickety, old wooden boat is docked at The Split; the Rastafarian captain occasionally takes tourist out for cruises. He also seems to be the local connection for the green leafy stuff they import from Jamaica. His friends, or make shift crew appeared stoned all day, and every day! Yes, life is pretty relaxed at The Split and on Caye Caulker.

Food

If you are a seafood lover Caye Caulker is for you. My first day's consumption consisted of some conch Ceviche, a whole Red Snapper, and popcorn lobster. Of course those were washed down by sampling the local beers that were quite descent and much cheaper than home....about 2 bucks each or 10 bucks for 6 in a bucket of ice at some places. We had no luck with the wines from the grocery stores, even the familiar brands. I thing storage and heat were the culprits. Some of the upscale restaurants offered up some tasty vintages but the prices were comparable to home. The local rum was dirt cheap and quite flavorful. Just about everything is imported on the island so you have to keep that in mind; if you want cheap, you have to go local. Signs are posted daily out front of the various restaurants advertising specials and the catch of the day.

We were on the island for a month and didn't try all the restaurants it had to offer. Some became our favorites and some we steered clear of, one *(Syd's)* in particular I got food poisoning from. I guess I learned not to order a burger from a place where everyone else ate and raved about the chicken. We rated all the places we tried but this is not the venue to replicate the list. Owners and menus change but I'd like to think I could easily recommend places like "Habaneros," "Tropical Paradise" *(lobster nachos were my favorite)* "La Cubana" *(pig roasted daily),* "Rose's," "Amore Café *"(for Breakfast),* and "Sandros" which became our favorite in the end. We even had four fresh lobsters delivered to our door one evening by "Benedict," "the self proclaimed lobster king." He had heard we were in the market so he delivered, killed and cleaned them right outside our door. I could go on and on about the food but it is something where everyone has different tastes and must experience it on their own.

I think atmosphere and ambience go a long way in making a unique or enjoyable dining experience. "Popeye's," was the closest little restaurant to our bungalow; I had arrived on the island a few days prior to Cathryn and I stopped at this little beachfront place for a couple beers before dinner. It was a very dark night, with no moon and a magnificent star-lit sky. There was a little wooden fishing boat tied to the pier just off shore. Its pastel blue color glowed in the starlight. I couldn't see the end of the wooden pier as it disappeared into the darkness. I looked out to where I could hear the waves crashing onto the reef about a mile offshore and I noticed a tiny mangrove island silhouetted by the starry sky. I couldn't help myself at that point in considering the meaning of life.

The Snorkel King

Along with fishing, diving and snorkeling are popular activities in Belize since it is protected by the second largest living barrier reef in the world, second only to the "Great Barrier Reef" in Australia. There are numerous companies that can accommodate you but one came highly recommended. We chose "Carlos Tours" for an afternoon snorkeling excursion. I have snorkeled all over the Caribbean Sea and a few other places in the world, but I was immediately impressed with the underwater slide show Carlos presented in the office. Carlos was to guide our trip which included three different places to snorkel.

Carlos checked our equipment before leaving the office and didn't charge extra to replace my mask with one of his or for our flippers. The excursion was $50 U.S. each. Our first stop was at least twenty minutes out to the reef, in the shallows where we saw lots of amazing colored coral and oodles of different kinds of fish. New to me was seeing a giant sea turtle up close, and a giant sting ray about 6' across in width. Carlos and his first mate kept us corralled and away from the sharp and dangerous coral.

Our next stop was to be the most amazing snorkeling I've done ever! It was called Shark Alley, and it wasn't long after we anchored that a group of at least a dozen Nurse Sharks showed up. I guess it helped that Carlos was feeding the group that ranged in size from 3' to at least 8' in length. When he told us to gear up we all just looked at each other, then we volunteered the group know-it-all and loud mouth. He didn't get eaten so we figured it was safe to join him in the water. Carlos played around with one shark in particular, about 6' in length. He softly petted the shark and then swam to the bottom with it. The shark just lay still on the bottom and Carlos picked it up in his arms, rolled it over belly-up, and surfaced with it in his arms. We were all invited to come and pet the shark.....way, way cool!!!

We made a third stop that really didn't matter to me since I figured we really couldn't top the last stop. Lunch was a stop at San Pedro on Ambergris Caye; we ate and strolled a bit there deciding we had made the wiser choice by staying on Caye Caulker. On the way back Carlos carved up some fresh fruit to the group. He had been taking his own underwater camera shots throughout the day, and he let us view the slideshow upon returning to his office. His photographic skills were just as amazing as his diving and shark handling capabilities. We downloaded and bought a copy of the slideshow; friends back home thought it was something taken and made by National Geographic.

The Bat Cave

Cave tubing is a sport quite common in Belize that I had never even heard of before. We've all heard of river rafting or river tubing but this was billed as different in that you actually floated down a river through mountain caves! The caves are about a 45 minute drive inland (*west*) towards Guatemala. There are plenty of travel agents on the island that can arrange the trip for you but we had our landlord set it up for us through one of her connections. We had to catch a water taxi to the mainland and Belize City where our guide Gustavo was waiting for us on the arrival platform. He whisked us off to an air conditioned car where his partner, the driver was waiting. Gustavo chatted, gave us our itinerary and taught us a history lesson as we drove.

The caves are in the Mayan Mountains where the river has eroded its way through the limestone. You get suited up on arrival with a life vest and a head lamp to strap on so you can see in the dark caves; there is mostly no light for the 45 minute journey. The inner tubes were yellow, with handles....the kind we use for tubing behind boats back home, and they actually import them from

Canada. Our guide was Louis, the driver of our car. Turns out he is a licensed guide who also does the cave tours. We didn't recognize him after he got into his swim gear and dumped his ball cap. We walked up a stone path that took us into the jungle. Louis proved he was quite knowledgeable as he explained and described the flora and fauna as we walked. It was about a 45 minute walk; I noticed how the jungle canopy above us was quite thin and Louis pointed up to some of trees where the tops had been ripped off by the last bad hurricane here.

The trail took us uphill on an easy grade and we eventually came to the river that would take us back down the mountain. The water was cool and very refreshing. The caves with their unique rock formations were quite impressive. While we were cooling ourselves down we noted hundreds of minnows swimming around us. Cathryn thought they were cute until they started biting her. Louis just laughed and said they nibble the dead skin from your body and that the Japanese use them for exfoliation. She didn't think she had any dead skin on her buttocks!

We mounted our tubes and strapped on our headlamps and Louis hitched us together with me behind C and my feet tucked under her armpits. Louis guided us out into the current that swept us into the cave and we switched on our lights. There were dozens of cliff swallows darting in and out of the cave mouth; Louis was impressed that I was the first person who actually knew they were swallows and not bats. Caves are caves, are caves and I've been in many of them over the years. These really didn't look much different except for the fact they weren't artificially lit and you were floating through them on an inner tube. It was very relaxing and pretty cool! There were the usual stalactites and stalagmites and some pretty cool formations that even looked like animals. We could see some fruit bats tucked up into holes in the cave ceiling.

We floated at different speeds throughout the cave depending on the current and some times Louis had to paddle for us or guide us around and over the rocks. At one point we could hear that notable sound of a waterfall ahead and Louis asked if we were ready. Louis guided us into the water fall, but he had fooled us since it was coming down on us, and we didn't have to go over any cliff; it was another underground spring emptying into the river. After about 30 minutes the river dumps you out of the cave into the open; you can see where the water gets really deep in some spots....up to 30 feet according to Louis. There were some spots where the high tides and raging water took trees the size of telephone poles and rammed them into the rocks or river banks. The river deposited us right back where we started and our cave experience came to a bitter sweet end.

"The breeze in Belize blew mainly in the trees."

Consider the Conch

Caye Caulker, Belize

Don't tell me how educated you are, tell me how much you traveled."

– Mohammed

A I walked around the island, the sand roads, trails, and beaches I noticed the usual things; including the conch shells that we all have seen before. They are those large, pink and beige shells you might have held up to your ear to hear the ocean, or perhaps saw in a "Tarzan" movie where the natives were using them as a horn to warn villagers of impending danger. Now think a little harder and try to remember where else you've seen them.

Consider this:

They lay in the water, sand, or along the beaches everywhere,
They are used to line gardens, paths, and up porch stair.

They're filler under docks, and in cement footings and wells,
They are polished or shined, to sell.

You can blow them as a horn.
Or carve them into jewelry, to adorn.

They are home for some hermit crabs,
There is meat inside that's edible and not too drab.

Pieces are placed on fence tops to keep out people and critters,
They are used in Ceviche, chowder, and fritters.

You can bang on them making music that rhymes,
Or string them together, to make wind chimes.

They are sacred in some ancient cultures,
Natives used them as breastplates, to prevent chest punctures.

They were worn on the hands as weapons to thump,
I could go on and on, like "Bubba" in "Forest Gump."

A conch and cheese omelet to munch,
Is just what I am craving for lunch!

Princess of Belize

Caye Caulker, Belize

"I have found out that there ain't no surer way to find out whether you like people or hate them than to travel with them."
— Mark Twain

The Arrival

Let me introduce you to my sweetheart Cathryn, or "Princess" as I call her *(we live together)*. She is a very attractive, outgoing, and social woman who always strives to look her best. She also likes to make an entrance and to grab your attention if she can, through her grace, and fashionable wardrobe. Only my princess would have a separate wardrobe planned for each flight, airport, and her eventual arrival in Belize. Whether it's a washroom, phone booth, or parked vehicle, she can change outfits quicker than Superman when he's about to save the world. This wardrobe change usually includes a dress, or blouse and skirt of some sort, and matching shoes, of course!

I had gotten to Belize a few days prior to my princess so I hired a cab to go and pick her up at the airport. Shortly after her plane's arrival I saw her in the Immigration line chatting away with the female Immigration agent. I thought she was getting the third degree but as it turns out the woman liked her hair and wanted to know how she does it and what kind of product she uses in it. Go figure, the guy that questioned me just wanted to know what I was going to do with myself for a whole month in Belize.

As I have come to expect, my princess turned heads as she strutted out the airport doors decked out in a flowery sundress, and lacy high-heeled sandals, showing just enough cleavage to get a free taxi ride…silly me for bargaining with the cab driver ahead of her arrival. Hector, my cab driver, just went completely silent after chewing my ear off non stop for the whole ride to the airport. Having some prior experience in staying cool and hydrated while in the tropics, I thought it only proper to welcome royalty with a six pack on ice in the back seat of the cab. Cheers Princess and Welcome to Belize!

On Caye Caulker I welcomed my princess to our humble bungalow on the beach. She fell in love immediately with the cute little, green and white, wood sided shack on stilts. It was basically a bachelor unit with the bathroom sectioned off, and all the amenities we needed to eat, sleep, and be comfortable. My princess has a thing for cute little things like "Barbie" and doll houses. She still has some of her childhood dolls and I finally snuck her old, beat up Barbie camper out to the garbage only a couple months ago. Our new home away from home was comfy, cute, and cozy, Cathryn was happy.

The Chicken Drop

I once did a trip to a resort on the Mayan Riviera in Mexico where one of the bars had swings for bar stools. Well, they have them in Belize too; you probably can't sue anyone in these 3rd world countries if you fall off them. The Bar is called "Bamboozle" and I caught my first Belize buzz there on my arrival. I thought it only fitting that I take my princess there on her first night. Well, it didn't seem to take long and Cathryn was getting "Bamboozled;" it could have been the long day and lack of sleep or maybe the bottomless glasses of a rum drink called "Lover's Paradise." Either way, she was swinging and singing for more.

There is a unique game in Belize called" The Chicken Drop. It runs twice a week at this particular bar. They use chicken wire to make a square pen on the floor, and have the numbers 1 to 100 inside. More chicken wire is laid over the top of the board; this is where the chicken walks. Everyone then buys tickets for a buck each until they are all sold. Now comes the shitty part; they toss a live chicken into the pen and let it walk on run around until it shits on a number. It's that simple....and quick it seems.....I really think the poor chicken was just scared "shitless" by all the screaming and yelling. If the chicken shits on your number you win the $100 bucks, and you get to clean the shit off the board!

The princess and I bought some tickets and squeezed into the boisterous crowd to watch the event. Cathryn jockeyed for a good viewing position since she was more vertically challenged than most of the crowd. An announcer calls out the action as the game goes on. The game was over within a couple minutes and the crowd around the pen dispersed quickly. Well, the entire crowd except for Cathryn...it seems she didn't remember there was a coconut tree behind her and she did her own version of the Princess Drop. The Announcer caught the additional action and called it to everyone else's attention by asking over the loud speaker if she was ok. Oh well, shit happens!

The Titanic

After getting Bamboozled we decided it was time to wobble home, but not without enjoying the great ocean breeze and beautiful moonlit night. We strolled hand in hand out on to one of the water taxi piers where the warm breeze gently blew our hair back; "ahhh" we both sighed simultaneously as we walked out to the end of the pier. The stars lit up the sky as we got away from the lights, and the moon glittered off the water all around us; it looked like someone had scattered thousands of diamonds across a black velvet sheet. At the end of the pier there is a set of two stairs used for boarding the water taxis. There are no railings, just the starry sky and dark Ocean. The princess perched herself up on the stairs, just like on the bow of the Titanic, her outstretched arms catching the wind as if she was about to take flight. It was one of those pure moments. In her brazen bravado she flipped her sundress up over her head, and bared her beautiful, bodacious breasts in the beaming, and brilliant moonlight. She held her panties high in the air like a ship's flag. I couldn't help but smile, as she made that moment her own! The two young guys we hadn't seen at the other end of the pier were smiling too.

The Wall

We still had a ways to walk after the Titanic adventure and I felt like a swim. It was way too dark and scary to go in the ocean so we needed a pool. It pays to be polite and social with the locals and to ask for swimming privileges that weren't included with our rental unit. Our landlord had said we were welcome to use the pool at a condo building they managed in the neighborhood. Our problem was the hour and that the place was all locked up. The pool looked very inviting but it was behind a five foot cement wall. I easily boosted my princess over but then I couldn't get my fat ass over on my own. I kept jumping up and sliding back down into the cactus garden with my bare feet.

I was getting battered and bruised but we couldn't help but laugh out loud at our failed efforts. Cathryn came back over the wall and we gave up...almost. I was determined to get over that wall and I found a little plastic table a couple doors down. We conquered the wall and went skinny dipping trying not to make noise and wake the residents of the condo building. It should have been a romantic moment but the chilly water made for some serious shrinkage. The depth of the pool was over Cathryn's head so we thought we better get out before she drowned.

Kissing Frogs

We made it back to our sugar shack where I nursed my wounds and cracked a bottled of cabernet sauvignon for a night cap. The wine was the end of us although my princess pretended her batteries were still fully charged. She was talking and yawning at the same time with her eyes closed. Just before lights out my princess took a knee beside the bed and produced a ring just like the one I have given her with a proposal of marriage at Christmas. She said that I was her special frog and she asked me to marry her. I said yes.

It was really a happy ending to Cathryn's first day in Belize, at least until her phone alarm went off at 3 am! The annoying alarm tone continued while my princess stumbled around the bungalow, throwing out f-bombs while she tried to find the phone. She finally found the phone but then couldn't turn it off. Her language got worse and she threatened to throw her phone in the lake. I kindly reminded her it was an ocean. Anyway, the alarm was silenced, a blissful sleep followed, and we are living happily ever after.

"She's not a real princess, but she's my princess!"

Caye Caulker Critters

Caye Caulker, Belize

"Traveling is physically tiring but mentally refreshing."
– Nitin Sharma

Geckos and Iguanas

You have to wonder some times how the hell certain things, such as various animals or critters get on to an island that is miles away from fresh water, bush, jungle, or other habitats that usually support these forms of life. Caye Caulker in Belize surely isn't unique in its collection of critters, but they do catch one's attention, especially for us northern city folk. Anyone who's been to Mexico or the Dominican on vacation has seen the little geckos that dart in and out of protection whenever we come near. I'm sure some of you have also seen the larger Iguanas in some other tropical places. I hadn't thought about it prior to my arrival, but it's always a bit startling when you come around a corner and there is a two foot long, prehistoric looking creature blocking your path. They don't seem to do much, and they really aren't too concerned with human presence; they just seem to like lying around in the sun.....kind of like most of us tourists I guess. Perhaps they too are from another land far off, and they have settled here for the hot climate.

Crabs

These critters are a little more skittish and elusive, for the most part. Everyone's seen those little guys on the beach that pop out in and out of the sand near the waters edge. I was more than curious here when I first walked about the island and saw holes all over the place, in the sand. They were of varying sizes; some reminded me of crayfish holes I found as a kid. We used to dig down into the ground until we found the crayfish, and then of course, bring them home to mom. I caught sight of a few of the crabs while I walked and they were a fair size, some as big as a plum. There were several holes under and around the cabin we were staying in so I just figured they were from the crabs or perhaps the Iguanas burrowed there. One afternoon I came back to the cabin to find my socks under the porch, they had been drying up on the railing. When I retrieved the one from under the porch I noticed it had been pulled down into one of these holes. I pulled it out of the hole and discovered that something had chewed though the toe of my sock!

One night just after it got dark, Cathryn and I were sitting on our veranda, and I saw something moving across our yard. At first I thought it was a leaf blowing across the sand; then I saw it was a huge crab, bigger than my outstretched hand, or around the size of a salad plate. He looked like he should be cooked, and on a plate for dinner. I got up to take a picture and then I saw another one following the other from under our cabin. I'm not sure how many of them were under there but I was glad they were there, and not in the cabin. From the holes I saw on this island, there's got to be a gazillion of them living there.

Cats and Dogs

It doesn't seem to matter where you venture to in the world; you always seem to run into cats or dogs. Caye Caulker is no different but it is not over run with the animals by any means. Many seem to be strays but I've also seen many of the dogs with collars on them. One night we saw two little kids come running through our yard chasing their dog that was running ahead of them dragging the rope he broke during his escape. A few days earlier I had come out of the shower to find an orange Tabby cat in my living room. He seemed to hang out in the neighborhood looking for hand outs here or at the Cuban restaurant across the street. There is one dog somewhere in the neighborhood that really pissed us off with the early morning barking, but you can have that enjoyment at home. For the most part the animals were well behaved and we saw quite a few brought right into the restaurants or bars with their owners.

Lobsters

If there is one creature I was pleasantly surprised with in Belize it was the lobster. On my first day of menu surfing along the main street I noted some kind of lobster dish at every restaurant. There was grilled whole lobster, or just the tails, stuffed lobster, lobster lasagna, lobster nachos, lobster soup, lobster poppers, and lobster salad. I saw some on an open grill and noted they are different than the north Atlantic kind I'm used to in that they have no front claws. They are called "Spiny Lobster" there in the Caribbean. The local price was about one third to one half of the price at home so I made it a point to sample as many of the dishes as I could. My favorite became the lobster nachos with a bucket of beer for lunch at the Paradise restaurant.....yum!

To my surprise one evening; I found that you can have whole, fresh lobster delivered right to your front door. It was just before dinner time one evening when we heard a guy outside of our cabin shout "hello." Standing by our front porch was a half Rastafarian looking dude, maybe more like an older version of Buckwheat from the Little Rascals. He was wearing only shorts and holding up 4 live lobsters in his hands. The man introduced himself as "Benedict," "The Lobster King." He said his buddy Pops told him we were looking for some lobster so he thought he'd drop by with some *(Pops was supposed to deliver two days prior but we were on "island time"*). Benedict said he wanted 15 bucks for all four of the crustaceans and we hadn't eaten yet so we agreed to take the critters off his hands, literally.

We weren't sure exactly what we were going to do with the lobsters since we didn't have a pot or grill to cook them in or on. Before we could even decide Benedict asked for a knife and said he'd clean them at no extra charge. He went to work right on top of out septic tank lid….like an above ground cistern. Benedict ripped the tails right off the live critters, split them up the middle so we could retrieve the meat, and he even discarded the remains in the nearby ocean so that they could be recycled by nature. Our neighbors Patty and Travis came out to see what was going on so we invited them over for some wine and a lobster appetizer before dinner. Cathryn went to work separating the meat from the tail shells and I cut it into bite sized chunks. I whipped up a garlic/mayo dipping sauce and she fried the meat up with some butter and garlic and a squirt of lime. She garnished the plate with some fresh kiwi and it was an appetizer from heaven that easily fed the four of us. Fresh, delicious, and way yummy!!!

The String Thing

This is a rare animal indeed; not only do I think it's exclusive to Belize, or more specifically to Caye Caulker, but I think that we may have had the only one in existence actually residing on our property! It was not really that visible at night, and seemed to be most active in the mid day heat. It was quite long and skinny, multi-colored, and it liked to hang out on our porch. Unbeknownst to me, Cathryn actually found and adopted this critter and brought it home where she played with it every day. She was talking about finding and keeping an animal like this since the day she arrived on the island. Hence, she was happy, finding the perfect spot on the porch to keep her new pet. I just shook my head since only a woman would adopt such a simple and silly pet of this type.

Cathryn called it a "clothes line." This was no normal clothes line to say the least; it was made up of no less than six different pieces of string and rope that she'd collected from the beach, or from garbage strewn along the roads and paths. She strung and pieced this string thing together for a week and then officially hung it on the porch and called it her own.

"That's my princess!"

Pops' Island

Caye Caulker, Belize

"Life is either a daring adventure or nothing."

– Helen Keller

Finding an Island

How does one find the perfect little island that you can call your own, a tropical island paradise to fish, snorkel, or just run around naked on if you feel the desire? Well, I first got the idea from a link on the Internet while I was researching a trip to Belize or the Honduras. There were a few private islands in the Honduras but none I could find near Belize. While emailing back and forth with the landlord of the place I rented in Belize, I ran the idea by her. Mariya, the landlord, knew of a local fisherman named "Pops," who took fishing charters to an island for lunch; she looked into it for me. When I got to Belize I worked on the plan with her; I wanted to surprise Cathryn when she arrived a few days later. Mariya asked Pops if we could do some fishing with him, catch dinner, and then stay on the island. In his package deals he would normally clean and cook your catch of the day on the island, then return you to Caye Caulker. So, for $200 U.S. Pops agreed to take us fishing, cook dinner for us, leave us on his private island for the night, and then pick us up the next day. It was as simple as that, although we were the first folks to ever make such a request. We do like to be different!

Pops

We were told that Pops would pick us up around "mid day" at our bungalow and take us to his boat. Cathryn figured that meant he'd be there at exactly noon but I knew better. We were on "Island time" while on Caye Caulker, I reminded her. We joked that Pops had to be some salty, old Rastafarian sea dog, with three good teeth. He promptly arrived at 12:30pm and proved us wrong; Pops was 30ish, clean cut, pretty buff, and very professional. We loaded up his golf cart and away we went. He made a few pit stops for some supplies, and he confessed to us that he couldn't find his first mate anywhere on the island. I told him I kinda had my sea legs, and I could maybe help him out a bit. He said that would be great if I could free dive to 30 feet, and help him scoop up some lobsters from the ocean bottom for dinner. 30 years and 90 pounds ago I would have tried something like that.....maybe!

Pops filled in the details of our excursion as we made our way to his boat, and then out to sea. The plan was to do some trolling and perhaps some still fishing to catch us some dinner; then we would check his lobster traps for an extra treat. We had heard that he was a great cook; he said he would clean our catch and cook us dinner on his private island, which had been in his family of fishermen for 3 generations.

Dinner

I've done a little fishing in my day and Cathryn assured me she loved it. Pops circled the boat around a sand bar out near his island, about 2-1/2 miles from Caye Caulker. He baited our lines and explained the trolling process to us. You let the lines out about 100 feet behind the boat, and then added a jigging motion. The princess *(Cathryn)* was tiring after a while, and neither of us had caught anything but sea grass. Pops said he'd give her another 5 minutes before he took over; he had "never" been shut out *(I've heard that before!)*. Sure enough, a minute later the princess was yelling; she landed one. It didn't give her much of a fight, but you could see there was some good weight on her line. She pulled in a barracuda, about 18 inches long and maybe 3 pounds. Pops thought it was a good eating size, but I asked him what he and Cathryn would be eating.

You would think I'd be next but C took another hit. She had been giggling how it was easier to grip the pole between her legs, but when the second fish bit, the fishing pole became quite intimate with her. The combination of the invasive fishing pole and landing a good fish panicked her; she accidentally released the lock button on her reel. This fish was a big one and it took off with the line. Pops grabbed the pole and swung it around the rear of the boat to give the fish some slack. He fought with the line and the fish until I could take it from him; he was also trying to steer the boat, and keep it in position. I brought in the fish and he grabbed it with a grappling hook. It was a feisty bastard; it flipped off the hook and on to Pops' feet where a tooth caught the side of one ankle. It was another barracuda, over two feet long and about 5 or 6 pounds....a beauty, and enough to complete our dinner entrée. Pops took the line back and tried to untangle the reel; it looked like a bowl of cooked Angel Hair pasta. He said, "This line is done." Cathryn apologized, and said to me we should give him a good tip! Pops only suffered a minor flesh wound from the fish bite.

The Lobster Hotel

They have different lobsters in the southern hemisphere; they're "Spiny Lobsters" and they don't have claws like their cousins of the North Atlantic. Pops had some traps laid out around his island so we cruised around trying to find them. I spotted a trap and he used the grappling hook to fetch it from the ocean bottom, maybe 12' to 15' down. The traps weight a ton *(with the added water pressure)* so I had to help him pull it in the boat. You could see some lobsters inside; a bunch of little crabs and fish spilled out onto the bottom of our boat. We checked the lobsters inside and they weren't big enough to eat. Pops said he'd leave them in there so they could call there bigger friends to visit.

He told us to keep our eyes peeled for his lobster hotel. The fishermen take a large piece of corrugated roofing material and lay it on the ocean bottom, 20 to 30 feet down. The lobsters hide underneath it; apparently they are just like us and they like a roof over their heads. Pops just wanted to show us one; it was a two man job evicting guests from the hotel, one guy to chase the guest out, and the other to catch it. I didn't think it was something I really needed to experience fist hand, just for the sake of eating lobster for dinner.

The Island

We bumped into another boat we had seen earlier on the way out of port; a cousin of Pops, and some other local stoners were aboard. The boat's captain was a weathered Rastafarian dude who wore only shorts, and a bad smile that showed his rotten teeth. His dreadlocks looked frosted from the salt air, and I doubt if they'd seen shampoo in years. To his credit, he had scored himself a young, hottie American tourist chick for the day. A conversation in Creole took place amongst the cousins; I got the drift they were meeting us at Pops' island so the cousin could jump aboard with us, and continue the lobster hunt. Both boats then docked at the island where we were immediately met by the island security. There were four guards on the island....Spike, Jasmine, Missy, and Blue; all dogs who have the run of the island when Pops is not there. They were all very friendly with the first two being some type of Pit Bull, Missy a type of Terrier one fifth of their size, and Blue, named by Cathryn since Pops had just brought him to the island, a puppy with no name.

Cathryn and I checked out the island and our accommodations, while one of the other guys started to clean our fish. There were two bunkhouses, 4 dogs, and an outhouse on the island....that's it! The island is basically a sand spit covered in mangroves, maybe a couple hundred feet wide, and a football field or so long. There was a cooking shack in between the cabins, and near the one dock. It was perfect! Things took a weird turn when we realized the other boat people weren't leaving, and the captain disappeared into the other cabin with his chicky. The cousin and his girlfriend were cleaning, and hovering around "our" fish; we got the impression they planned on staying for dinner. This would not do! The princess called Pops over for a word; she told him we were paying him for what had so far been a great day, and that these pirates were not an acceptable part of the package. We voted them off the island, and Pops asked them to leave.

Sharks!

The coolest and yet scariest thing that happened while the pirates were cleaning the fish was when they threw the guts in the water, and a six foot Nurse Shark came to dinner. The water beside the dock is only about 2 feet deep; this beast took its dinner, and then flipped over, splashing the dock with water on its way back out to sea. Pops said they were regular visitors, not to worry, and that the shark would be back later. He was right; Spike barked when the shark cruised back in, near the end of the dock. While the dogs and I were on shark patrol, Pops went to work prepping our dinner. By the time we sat down and got into a bottle of wine, he had some plantain fried up for us as an appetizer.

Pops had marinated and seasoned the fish, and was now cooking some in coconut oil. Since he couldn't produce a lobster, he surprised us by spearing a Cowfish from the pen he had beside his dock; apparently he had caught it some other time, and saved it for us. He said it was the chicken of the sea, and it really did taste "just like chicken." He cut the barracuda into steaks and fillets, and whipped up some coconut rice, and salsa. I sat there in awe watching him dice up the onions and tomatoes in the palm of his hand, with a fillet knife; the rest of us mortals use a cutting board! The meal was one of the best fresh fish feasts we've ever had; all from a guy who taught himself how to cook just because it's a way of life there.

Dancing the Night Away

Pops made a fire, and had "Ziggy Marley" playing over his solar powered, and battery operated sound system. The music engulfed the island. I walked Pops out to the dock, and his boat, while Cathryn went to put on some of our own music. I watched Pops' boat disappear into the darkness; when I turned around I saw Cathryn naked as the day she was born, dancing to "Moby." I stripped down to join her, like we were Adam and Eve on our own Paradise Island. There were only 3 light bulbs on the island, and we turned them off to enjoy the show; the Milky Way and its gazillions of stars lit up the sky like a giant fireworks display. The stars, "Moby," "Pink Floyd," "Enigma," and the ocean breeze, made us giddy; we laughed, and danced naked under the stars like two kids without a care in the world.

The dogs stood guard for us when we bedded down for the night; Spike slept on the top step of the bunk house, Blue whined to come in, then curled up on the floor near our bed. The gentle ocean breeze blew through the open doors and windows. At one point during the night, the wind picked up and we had to physically hold on to our bed sheets. The galaxy of stars acted as our night light. Mother Nature called on me during the night, and all I had to do was to stand in the doorway and pee into the ocean! Besides, the outhouse was a bit of a walk, and a little scary in the dark. It was like any other wooden outhouse, but you had to literally "walk the plank" to get to it. It was out, on the water; the ocean was the flush mechanism, and the marine life took care of recycling.

I don't usually get up before the crack of 9 but things were different on the island. We had enjoyed the sunset on the west side of the island, so it only made sense to watch the sunrise on the east side. We had no clocks, watches or even a cell phone with us, so we had no idea what time it was. Pops' fresh water supply was a huge black cistern that would get heated by the sun during the day. This water was used for our morning sponge bath, and to brush our teeth. I went for a stroll with the security team, watching them hunt in the mangroves. Cathryn cooked up some breakfast for us, and we couldn't stop smiling at each other while we ate; we just beamed over the beauty, and bliss of our own private paradise.

After breakfast we decided to do some snorkeling around the east dock where the shark had been. Pops said there were some starfish and seahorses in that area. Spike swam with us, staying on shark patrol. He circled around and kept close by, like our own secret service agent. Pops had told us he'd be back around "mid day" to pick us up, so we just chillaxed, trying out the hammocks and enjoying the solitude. Just before Pops came back for us, a fishing charter buddy of his stopped by with some clients. We heard the boat coming and realized we were still naked, so we thought we'd better get dressed. It was funny how it we felt like the visit was an intrusion, but it was just our reminder that our time in paradise was coming to an end.

One last, crazy event that took place on the island was when the new arrivals were cleaning their fish, and the shark came back. Spike had been standing guard on the end of the dock, and then he jumped right in the water almost landing on top of the shark, scaring it away. Pops said the dog has been bitten before;

obviously Spike would have no problem taking a bullet for the president!

"Just another day in Paradise"

In The Jungle

Tikal and Flores, Guatemala

"Twenty years from now you will be more disappointed by the things you didn't do than by the ones you did do. So throw off the bowlines, sail away from the safe harbor. Catch the trade winds in your sails. Explore. Dream. Discover."

– Mark Twain

Central America

Why Belize? Guatemala? I was asked that particular question on more than one occasion before, and after my trip there. To explore, dream, and discover as Mr. Twain put it. From the time of my first adventure, I always said I wanted to travel, "while I still can." Let me list some of my other personal reasons for travelling to third world countries such as these: cheap, exotic, historic, architectural, people, food, nature, ruins, jungle, and memories.

I had been curious about Belize for a few years prior to the trip there, and I've always been interested in Mayan, Inca, or Aztec ruins. So the plan was to stay on Caye Caulker, Belize, and to try and see some Mayan ruins sites on the mainland. A side trip to Tikal, Guatemala was a must, while we were "in the neighborhood." Tikal is arguably the largest excavated Mayan ruin site in Central America, along with Chichen Itza. Having seen and thoroughly enjoying the latter, I looked forward to discovering the similarities, and/or differences in the Tikal site. Cathryn and I ventured to Caye Caulker and made ourselves at home for a month.

Making a Plan

Trying to book an organized tour or even a self-guided trip to Tikal and Guatemala from Belize was an adventure in itself. Cathryn and I spent at least a few days chatting with various travel agents on Caye Caulker, trying to customize a trip to our liking. Flight prices from the island were ridiculously over-priced, with complicated schedules. Buses were doable but it would be a grueling full day ride through rural Belize and Guatemala, with not much to see en route. We looked into using the same guide, who took us cave tubing in Belize, but the Border was an obstacle, and guides could not cross from one country into the other.

I had been on all kinds of crazy bus adventures on previous trips; in this case I wanted to keep things a bit more simple, organized, and stress-free for Cathryn's first trip into a real third world country, with a different currency, language, and substandard transportation system. We finally agreed on taking the water taxi to Belize City, where we'd hop on a local bus that would take us to the Guatemala border. A Guatemalan Guide was to meet us at the border, then take us to the Tikal ruin site, with a possible side trip to the town of Flores, either before or after the ruins. That was the plan.

Boat, Bus, and Border

I had already used the water taxi between Belize City and Caye Caulker a few times so it was not big deal, I thought. To make the early bus on the mainland we had to catch the first water taxi; that meant getting up a little earlier than my usual crack of nine. Since I had never really ventured out that early, I didn't know how busy the first water taxi would be. They never seem to "sell out" these things, but I could see the line contained way more people than the boat was going to hold, or so I thought. My thoughts then turned to concerns when we boarded the boat, and our luggage did not. "No problem" we were told, our luggage would meet us there. I thought about the feasibility of that statement since there was no other boat in sight. We packed ourselves into the boat, like a tin of sardines; I foolishly thought we might have been able to sit up top, but some ignorant local guys jumped the line, and helped themselves to the prime seats.

We got to Belize City and confirmed that our luggage was in fact, not on our boat. A porter sent us to the ticketing area where there was another cart full of luggage. To this day I do not know how on earth our luggage arrived there ahead of us. We scooped our bag and waited for the bus; not to my surprise, the bus was delayed. A beat up old tour bus, finally pulled in about 45 minutes late; an elderly American couple immediately went into a tirade over the fact they were promised a shiny, comfortable, air conditioned bus like the one they saw in the brochure. I just chuckled, and said, "Welcome to Belize." I am a pretty large guy and I could not wedge myself into my assigned seat unless I totally reclined the broken backrest. The bus was less than half full, so we tried out different seats as we got underway. The only seats that were compatible to my large frame were at the back of the bus, where the "conditioned air" did not reach. Such is life on the bus.

As I thought, the bus ride was boring and uneventful; we managed to catch a few winks to compensate for our early morning rising. The bus brought us to the end of the line at the border of Guatemala. There, we had to disembark and walk through Customs and Immigration. For anyone who's been to a third world country, you know what this means: everything moves very slowly, and it is all done by hand! There are no computers, or scanners, our names were hand written into a huge ledger at Immigration. Customs requested that we pay some type of "conservation fee," on top of our "entrance fee" in to the country. No one could tell us why we had to pay the extra fee, you just do it, or you don't get in the country. I'm sure it went into someone's pocket.

We were over an hour late arriving; to my surprise, our guide was standing at the gate, waving at us. The guide introduced himself with a Spanish name we just couldn't comprehend so we settled on "Emilio." We were immediately swarmed by a group of men waving huge bundles of paper money; these were the Currency exchange Dudes. I Looked to Emilio hoping to trust his advice; he told us they offered a fairly competitive exchange rate. He also told us there was an exchange booth on site where we could change our American or Belizean Dollars into Guatemalan Quetzals. Cathryn had stashed some U.S. cash in our travel bag, so she searched for it while the Currency exchange Dudes hovered around us. The heat of the day and horde of sweaty men freaked Cathryn out and she shouted, "Stand back, and leave me alone!"

Boosted

An exhaustive search for our U.S. cash came up empty; we came to the realization we had ripped off. We figured it had to be during the only time our bag was out of our sight, when we were on the water taxi. It was less than $200 bucks and Cathryn learned a valuable lesson in not stashing cash in your bag. I still had some Belizean bucks and my credit cards, so I told Emilio we'd need to find a bank machine if he wished to get paid for his services. I told Cathryn shake it off; I've found out from previous bad experiences that you try to forget about it and move on, or the event will consume you, and ruin your trip. Negativity only begets negativity, so I just chalk it up to experience and move on. Such is the life of a seasoned traveler.

Tikal

Emilio walked us to his van; I chuckled at the look of horror on Cathryn's face as we climbed in through the side door. Emilio's chariot was a classic I'm sure...maybe 20 years and 400,000 miles ago! I couldn't discern the make or model because of the replacement parts of different shapes and colors. The van was ten times more beat up than the bus I had bitched about earlier, but there was lots of room inside for the two of us to spread out. I told Emilio his van looked good for such an "old" vehicle. He smiled and assured me it was in top mechanical form. He admitted he was in need of a new van, but he had to pay for his children's education first. I told Cathryn not to worry since we'd have no problem differentiating Emilio's van from all the other newer, plain white tour vans we saw on the road.

We discussed our plan with Emilio to visit Tikal, and maybe Flores, while we motored down the road with the air conditioning cooling us off. Emilio's van was equipped with "fifty-air:" This is where you roll down all the windows and go fifty miles an hour to get air. In any case, the moving air was a relief from the sweltering heat and humidity that we had picked up as we moved further inland. Emilio said we would arrive too late in the day to have enough time to tour the ruins at Tikal; he suggested staying in the area over night, and then touring the park the next morning. It seemed we had either miscalculated, or that we had been misinformed about the distance, and time it would take to get to Tikal. We thought we could stay in Flores and visit Tikal from there, but Emilio said it wasn't feasible with the distances involved.

The ride got more interesting as we cruised though the small villages, and the jungle on both sides of the road grew thicker, and closer. The yellow road signs that warn you of sharp curves and such, started to warn us of snake or cougar crossings; something we don't see too much of at home in the city! Cathryn and I had been discussing our options on whether to go to Tikal or Flores first, when Emilio said, "the fork" in the road was just ahead and he needed a decision. "On to Tikal" I said; Emilio nodded, and complied. He said he knew of a couple places just outside of the gates of the national park where we could stay for the night. This was really our best option since we were late into the afternoon already.

The forest and/or jungle all around the ruins at Tikal is under the protection of a national park. At the park gates there were a couple of restaurants, across the road from each other. The gate to the park looked like "it" was in ruins, and there were guards with automatic weapons on site. Emilio wandered off to find us a park guide, and we sat down for a well deserved, cold beer. A couple of "Gallo" (pronounced Guyo) beers about half the size of Cathryn were promptly delivered to our table with a menu. We consulted another group of tourists at the next table about our lunch selections. They had just been zip-lining as part of their package tour. The lines actually ran right from the restaurant we were at, up, and into the jungle.

We were enjoying our chicken enchilada with some local green veggies called "cho cho" when Emilio returned, and introduced us to our park guide. I didn't note, and can't recall his name but he was a slight man who spoke softly and reminded me of a history teacher. In contrast, he looked more native Guatemalan than Emilio, who was well over six feet tall, and built like a brick shithouse. The guide agreed to meet us near our hotel in the morning; he suggested we wait until after 4pm to buy our tickets to enter the park since they'd charge us for two days if we didn't.

Somehow, Emilio got us two tickets about an hour before that, and the armed guard waved us through.

Jungle Accommodations

Emilio said he could get us into "The Jungle Lodge," right at the entrance to the ruins for $100 U.S. a night. That is pricey for Guatemala but the location was super convenient, and we pay more than that at home in some places. The hotel was set right in the jungle, and it was beautiful. The rooms were spread out, secluded, clean, and quiet. I was just inspecting the room when Cathryn shouted, "There's a monkey in the tree!" Apparently we were sharing the jungle with Howler and Spider monkeys. I didn't see it. We went for a walk to check out the pool before dinner and Cathryn spotted another monkey; all I saw were the tree branches moving. Dinner was delicious; I had the best beef Carpaccio ever, and we both had superb steak dinners. In contrast to Belize, Guatemala is known for their excellent quality beef. They had an impressive wine list, and the meal was surprisingly cheap for a fancy hotel. Besides one group of tourists from a bus tour, we pretty well had the place to ourselves.

As we retired for the night Cathryn asked me why there was mosquito netting draped over, and around the beds. I wasn't really sure myself since all the windows were screened. Her question was soon answered when she went in the bathroom to brush her teeth; there, on the shiny white tiled floor was the biggest black spider we had ever seen! I had seen tarantulas before but this one was skinnier and somehow scarier looking. We weren't sure if we should kill it, or photograph it first, so we did both at the same time. The spider was at least four inches across! After I smashed it with my shoe Cathryn made me flush it down the toilet, and then barricade all the door bottoms with towels. We slept under the bug netting!

The Ruins

Our park guide was waiting for us after we finished our scrumptious breakfast, and off we went. We weren't into the park more than a couple hundred yards when we heard the Howler monkeys in the trees above. Finally! I saw a couple monkeys chasing each other, swinging on vines just like Tarzan, through the tree tops. Their commotion above caused a shower of leaves that fluttered down on us, flickering in the early morning sunlight. We heard other weird sounds from colorful parrots, and birds in the trees above, and around us. I stumbled over the tree roots along the dirt path while my eyes were scanning the trees above; "We weren't in Kansas anymore!"

After walking for awhile, we stopped and the guide asked, "Do you want me to take a picture of you here?" Cathryn and I had been looking everywhere except behind us, where the guide was pointing. Towering over us there was a fifteen storey, stone pyramid, framed by the lush green jungle. This was to be our first harmonious outburst of "WOW!" for the morning. The guide told us this was the back of one of the main temples in the Grand Plaza; it was just a tease for what was to come.

Around the corner of that temple, past some smaller structures, we walked into the Grand Plaza; it was like going back in time, going from the jungle, into an ancient city with mind boggling buildings and temples. The architecture was amazing! In a nutshell, the Mayans settled in the area around 800 BC, built their cities, and flourished until about 700 AD when they mysteriously abandoned their great cities. Similar Mayan cities like Tikal are scattered all over Central America, and into Mexico. It is also a mystery as to why the Mayans, Inca, and Egyptians all built cities in similar fashion in completely different parts of the world, without having any knowledge of each other!

Our guide walked us around the different buildings and temples of the Grand Plaza, explaining what we were looking at, and what the Mayan's were all about. The park covers about 222 square miles but only 10 square miles have been excavated. It took 13 years to excavate what is now visible, after the jungle swallowed it up when the inhabitants left. Exactly why the Mayans built such a city in the middle of a jungle is another mystery; the huge stones used to construct the 120 to 140 foot temples had to be quarried elsewhere, and then hauled to the site. We climbed one of the huge temples, perched ourselves near the top, and paused in awe. You can see other mounds scattered throughout the jungle where more temples remain buried, but you can only attempt to imagine this once great city.

Flores

As promised, Emilio was waiting outside the park gates upon our return from the ruins. We were curious as to where he had spent the night and next day when he was not with us. He later told us he drove the two hours back home to be with his family, and then he came back for us. Once we factored in his gas, time, and food, I don't know how the guy really made any money off us. We had not yet gotten to a bank machine, so we had to borrow some "expense money" back from Emilio *(that we had given him earlier)* to pay our park guide. It all worked out somehow. Emilio made a pit stop at some tourist trap on the road to Flores. We figured he knew the guy, as they always seem to know each other. We had no interest in souvenirs, but I obliged and bought an ice cream. Emilio turned the key but the van's battery was deader than a door nail. I watched him fiddle and fuss around while the heat and humidity forced us out of the van. I suggested we push start his chariot and Emilio waved out some manpower from inside the store. We pushed and he dropped her into gear; she fired up and bellowed thick blue smoke. Cathryn just howled and said I was her hero!

Emilio drove us to Flores, where a tiny island is joined to the mainland by a causeway that you drive over. Driving from the mainland to the island is like driving back a hundred years in history. There is a bank machine in the brand new shopping mall, and a Burger King at the entrance to the causeway. Once on the island there is nothing of the sort. There are outer and inner circular roads to navigate around the island. Emilio stopped at a couple different hotels and we settled on the "Casa Amelia" for $45 U.S. a night, including breakfast, Internet, real air conditioning, and a hot shower. Our room had a beautiful view of the lake, and there was a rooftop terrace with a view of the neighborhood. We bid farewell to Emilio and wished him well.

We explored the neighborhood and found a great little patio overlooking the lake. I can't tell you the name of the place, but the waiter's name was Norbert and he kept the coolies coming. Cathryn and I are "foodies" and at times, can be particular about what we like to eat. The cheeseburger was one of the best I've ever had! They used an amazing cheese that seemed to be repeated on Cathryn's mega-platter of nachos. An afternoon nap and some nookie made it a perfect afternoon! We scoped the hood for a dinner place and found "Raices Grill;" it had a beautiful patio right on the water. The patio was nicely lit with flowers spilling over half walls, and windowsills. Colorful wooden boats were tied up along the dock below the patio.

A Chilean cabernet sauvignon went superbly with my beef kabob. Cathryn chose a whole, local whitefish that was plenty tasty, but she didn't enjoy picking through all the bones. Another bottle of wine on our roof top patio led to more x-rated adventures in the bedroom. Plans are made to be changed, and we had only planned on being there a day before heading back to Belize. In consideration of our accomplishments and the mood Flores put us in; we decided to stay another full day.

We had nothing in particular to do, and all day to do it. A morning stroll revealed the true colors of Flores. The pastel colored buildings glowed in the early morning light. I went crazy with my camera, getting all those "post card" shots of colorful doors, windows, and the lake. We did a little boat tour around the lake where the boat acts as a ferry, stopping at other little villages along the lake to carry people across. We strolled, and nibbled on some fried Jack, a local street food. For lunch we went back to see Norbert and split a chicken quesadilla. Cathryn said the guacamole was "the best" ever! A little naked rugby in our room and then a siesta ended another perfect day!

We took a stroll on the other side of the island before dinner and found the "Cool Bean Café." They had a great patio overlooking the lake, with lots of trees, plants, and shade to chill out in. We enjoyed a cocktail, and watched a chicken strutting around in the bushes; we couldn't have been more relaxed and content. We tried a place called "La Luna" for dinner. The ambiance was great and the food was a perfect match. Some wine, a cheese and chorizo plate, then a steak for me and Roulade for Cathryn; "Wow" was the notation in her journal.

The next morning we had a taxi take us to the airport so we could fly back to Belize. We opted for the air travel to save our asses from another grueling bus ride, and to get a higher perspective of the countryside from the air. We barely put a dent in Guatemala as far as seeing the country, but the bit that we did see was truly amazing and completely rewarding.

"I wonder if the ruins of our civilization will ever be as interesting and amazing as the Mayan's."

Southern Comfort

Southern States, U.S.A.

"For my part, I travel not to go anywhere, but to go. I travel for travel's sake. The great affair is to move."
— *Robert Louis Stevenson*

Heading South

To head south from my home in Windsor, Ontario, Canada I have to cross the United States Border in Detroit Michigan. For many years before 9-11 this was a mere formality that cost less than a dollar and only a few minutes of your time chatting with a friendly border guard. Inflation and corporate greed have raised the cost of the crossing by bridge or tunnel to 5 bucks. Terrorism and illegal immigration have resulted in the mandatory presentation of a passport or an "enhanced driver's license" at all U.S. border points. The previously simple questions from polite customs officers has turned into a Gestapo type interrogation where you have to submit to a barrage of pointed questions about your destination, the reason for going there, and how much cash you are carrying to get there. The questioning gets even more personal but I won't whine any further in the interests of U.S. national security. You are left with the impression that the U.S. just doesn't want you in there country....whether you're travelling, or shopping and willing to spend your money there.

South side of the Ohio

On this particular trip our destinations were further south than southern Michigan and most of Ohio. Most of the first day was taken up by travelling south through Ohio along Interstate 75. I don't usually like riding my motorcycle on the Interstates but they do serve a purpose when you want to get somewhere directly and quickly. Anyone who travels this corridor usually boogies right through Ohio and into southern Kentucky before considering bedding down for the night. Since we were in no particular hurry to get anywhere and weren't interested in seeing anything until Cincinatti we did the Interstate thing until the first Kentucky exit off the bridge that crosses the Ohio River, separating Ohio and Kentucky.

You exit into the City of Covington and if you continue a few minutes east you're in Newport, Kentucky. As far as I'm concerned these are undiscovered gems that most people aren't even aware of. We later met a couple from Boston who told us we must be mistaken about the area we bragged of since Ohio and Kentucky don't share a border! It's pretty sad when Canadians have to give Americans geography lessons on their own country. These two towns offer a great view of Cincinnati from their side of the river and are linked to the metropolis by a few completely different style bridges, one of which you can safely walk across.

Much of downtown Newport is littered with beautiful historic buildings and houses on quiet shady streets. The levy along the river is lined with trendy bars and restaurants with great river and Downtown Cincinnati views. I had visited this area twice previously and was so taken by it I had to bring my significant other to see it on this occasion. Hotels are cheaper on the Kentucky side of the border and offer better views of Downtown Cinci. The communities are also linked together by a shuttle that runs by your hotel every 15 minutes and it only costs a buck. The night we were there the Cincinnati Reds were playing and many fans stayed south of the river and commuted across for the game. Ironically these two Kentucky settlements are included in "downtown Cincinnati" when you surf online for hotels.

Cathryn and I took the shuttle from our hotel over to downtown Cinci and got off in the heart of the city at a big square lined with shops, restaurants and bars. There was a band playing on a stage set up in the square; apparently this is a nightly thing throughout the summer. We sampled a few local craft beers along with some delicious appetizers in a couple of the places there. Another buck and trolley ride got us back to Newport where we strolled along the levy checking out the shops and restaurants. We perched ourselves on the patio of an Irish pub with a perfect night view of Cincinnati. The ball park lights lit up the river and the boats anchored there waiting for a foul ball or the forthcoming fireworks. We were treated to a fantastic free fireworks display after the game. My own city with our expansive waterfront should take notice of this place!

Honky Tonk

I have travelled the southern states extensively over the years but never ventured into Nashville, Tennessee. I suppose if I was a bigger country music fan I would have gone there sooner. Conversations with and recommendations from friends headed us to the country music capitol of the world. The popularity of the music and a huge concert downtown meant that we had to stay about six miles outside the city at a beat up "Howard Johnsons." Not much southern hospitality was to be had from a place run by a family from Pakistan.

Downtown Nashville was worth seeing, especially the streets "Broadway," and "Second Avenue." "Broadway" is a bit dirty looking from the thousands of tourists who stroll up and down the street day and night, where each and every bar has some sort of live entertainment. "Second Ave." was more pleasant for strolling with its tree lined sidewalks and seemingly more upscale restaurants and bars. Music is the theme in this city whether it is country or otherwise. We took in a "Nora Jones" concert at the

"Ryman Theatre" while we were there; a great venue for an intimate concert. This is where the couple from Boston told us Ohio and Kentucky are not anywhere near each other. Two taxi drivers recommended a restaurant called "Demos." The food was absolutely delicious and two steak dinners with a bottle of wine rung in at less than $50! You can also find great smoked ribs at "Rippy's Smokin Bar & Grill." It was here Cathryn got hooked on "Yeungling" beer, from America's oldest brewery.

Southern Hospitality

I actually Googled this term to get the true meaning of the words. True examples defining this term have been witnessed by all of us in the old movies where either someone breaks down in the middle of nowhere and is invited into a strangers house, or when the lone cowboy rides up to someone else's campfire and is offered a coffee or a meal. On several occasions we were witness to this tradition carrying on in the south. It is a little embarrassing at times being the recipient of these gestures knowing that we could have extended these same courtesies ourselves but have somehow been programmed not to. In some big cities just making eye contact with another person can get you shot.

It can be the simple gestures that are still appreciated; a man cutting his lawn at the roadside stops to let us pass without the possibility of grass or stones being ejected at us. Other folks cutting the grass or out gardening would wave at us as we passed by. Slower moving vehicles on scenic roads would actually pull to the right to let us pass by. People would stop and ask if we needed help if we pulled over to check our map or take a drink of water. A fellow biker frantically waved us over at a rest stop on the "Blue Ridge Parkway" to offer us half of a freshly cut watermelon. I thought he was broken down and needed help.

The temperature was over a hundred degrees and I pulled into a gas station for fuel and refreshment. The clerk saw how hot Cathryn was, went to the cooler, pulled out and opened a full bag of ice, and told her to help herself in filling our water bottle. At one of our hotels we entered the elevator with another couple and the woman commented on the bottle of wine I was holding. Sweaty and worn from the road I told her I'd gladly trade it for a cold beer. They invited us up to their room where they had beer on ice. We drank the cold beer over introductions and they refused to take the wine in trade. Cathryn commented that she just couldn't believe how nice people had been to us and she swore to make efforts to be a better person. Lesson learned.

Taking the Scenic Route

I truly appreciate how in the U.S. they actually build roads for the pure enjoyment of driving them. The "Blue Ridge Parkway" I mentioned is only one of them. On this particular trip I didn't have to point out the differences to Cathryn. We were making up some time on I77 from Virginia to West Virginia and the highway is fairly curvy and scenic as it winds through the mountains. Around the state line there is a tunnel that runs about two miles or at least the length of the song "T.N.T." by "AC/DC." The song blared from the radio as we entered the dark tunnel wedged between the rock wall on the left and a huge truck on the right. Doing 65 miles per hour in a dark curved tunnel in those circumstances was memorable to say the least. Cathryn had the song resonating in her head the rest of the day. *(She also shared it out loud a few times)*

In contrast I can't remember how many times Cathryn said "Wow" out loud as we drove the ridges of mountain tops with spectacular never ending panoramic views appearing at every other bend in the road. I know I always smile to myself when I'm winding my way along a quiet river valley road under tree canopies, feeling the cooler air from the moving water and trees and taking in the fresh scents of flowers or pine. On most of these roads you share it with no one a lot of the time. The older U.S. highways were built when people weren't in any particular hurry to get anywhere and there was less traffic. For me, these roads have become the scenic arteries of the U.S.

We booked a cabin outside Gatlinburg for a couple nights; it was a perfect little place with a deck that included a hot tub and a babbling brook running below. Sitting in the water with a cold beer gave us a better appreciation of the Smoky Mountains. I've been to Gatlinburg and Pigeon Forge many times and have become determined to stay away from the main road that runs through the cities. The continuous heavy traffic congestion and tacky tourist attractions eventually forced the true local artists into the hills outside town.

U.S. 129

I like to seek out new roads and destinations on every trip but I also wanted to let Cathryn experience the thrill of such roads as U.S. 129, better known as the "Dragon's Tail." Some of the roads leading to and around U.S. 129 are more scenic but the "Dragon's Tail" is famous to driving enthusiasts riding motorcycles or in cars. The road is challenging to any driver with its 311 curves in its 11 mile length. Photographers wait along the route snapping your photos that you can later retrieve via the internet. A place called "Deals Gap" lies around the unofficial half way point. You can get a room, gas, food, or a souvenir t-shirt there. There is even a "Tree of Shame" in the parking lot where pieces of crashed bikes hang from the branches. Upon departing Deals Gap Cathryn said she now felt like a real "Biker Bitch."

Edmond Gagnon

The Biltmore

"The Biltmore," in Asheville, North Carolina, is billed at the largest house in North America. It rivals many European mansions and sits on 8,000 acres of manicured and forested land. The main house is 2 miles from the front gate! The estate is actually the origin of the U.S. Forestry Service. George Vanderbilt visited various European palaces before having his own place built for him and his wife from 1889 to 1895. It was fitted with electricity and hot water heat. There is an elevator, bowling alley and indoor pool. The entire library ceiling complete with a mural was purchased from an estate in Europe, transported in 13 pieces and installed on site. The family still runs the place and you can tour it for the measly sum of $55 each! They have added a huge winery and Inn since my last visit over 20 years ago. The place truly is amazing and is worth seeing even at the ridiculous cost. Money was not an object when this place was built!

Mother Nature

I'm not really sure where the south ends anymore but scenic U.S. highways can still be found to take you north. On my last two trips I have found some back roads in Ohio that are truly a bikers dream. Although Mother Nature provides beautiful landscapes to titillate our senses, she can also be very destructive in altering some of the same landscape. On this particular trip she provided a huge storm to try and quell the heat wave sweeping across southern Ohio and West Virginia. We missed most of the storm while secure in our motel room but others were not so lucky. We witnessed how powerful our mother can be the next day heading north into Ohio.

At first we just noticed tons of leaves blown from the trees along with some small branches. Then we noted that the traffic

206

lights were out as well as the power in the towns we drove through. There were huge trees that had been completely uprooted or snapped off at the base and laying across vehicles or houses. We heard on the radio that 1 million homes were without power and the Governor was declaring a state of emergency. Almost all of the debris had been moved from the roads during the night so we really didn't feel affected by the storm, until we needed gas.

Most stores as well as the gas stations were all shut down making most towns look deserted. After receiving some directions from a very tired hydro guy we made a detour to a town away from our intended route in search of gasoline. The guy said there was one station in the town and his wife had waited an hour and a half for gas. Not having any choice we headed for the town of Glouster. We found a grocery store along the way and thought we'd better find something to eat there. The store was running off a generator and all perishables had been removed from the shelves. Fritos and warm cheese dip would be our lunch.

We found the gas station in Glouster with about 80 cars waiting in line for gas and only one pump in operation. After waiting in a stagnant line in the sweltering heat for about a half hour I decided to seek gas elsewhere. We had been told there was another town about 20 miles away with gas. I had less than a quarter tank and thought we might just make it. Five miles into the trip my reserve light came on. The engine moaned and groaned a bit as I coaxed it up the hills and then coasted down. I counted the miles down trying to figure how far we'd have to walk. I had to be running on fumes as they say when we cruised into the town of McConnelsville. There were only about 20 cars in line for gas here so we lucked out.

"It's unfortunate you have to travel so far south, for southern hospitality."

And the adventures continue…

CPSIA information can be obtained at www.ICGtesting.com
Printed in the USA
LVOW07s2138111013

356571LV00001B/7/P